Sermons for the Seasons

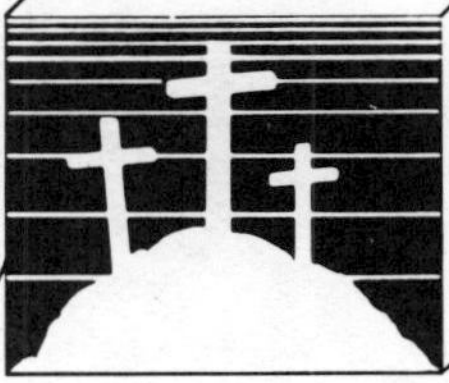

SERMONS for the SEASONS

C. W. BESS

BROADMAN PRESS
Nashville, Tennessee

To my wife Mary

4222-56

ISBN: 0-8054-2256-0
Dewey Decimal Classification: 252.6
Subject Heading: SERMONS—COLLECTED WORKS
Library of Congress Catalog Number: 84-23226

Printed in the United States of America

Unless otherwise stated, all Scripture references are from the Revised Standard Version of the Bible, copyrighted 1946, 1952, © 1971, 1973.
Scripture quotations marked KJV are from the King James Version of the Bible.

Library of Congress Cataloging in Publication Data

Bess, C. W., 1942-
Sermons for the seasons.

1. Occasional sermons. 2. Sermons, American.
I. Title.
BV4254.2.B47 1985 252'.6 84-23226
ISBN 0-8054-2256-0 (pbk.)

Contents

3. Celebration of Daily Living

Acknowledgments

How does a river recognize and acknowledge its many sources of water? Mine is the same impossible task of thanking all who contributed ideas and encouragement for this book.

Mary, my marriage mate for life, patiently typed many manuscripts for this project. Only with her insight and suggestions did the outline ever take form. Words can never convey my love and appreciation to this one who shares my life. In the truest sense it's our book together.

At home son Craig and daughter Kristen provided sympathetic support ("Dad, shouldn't you be busy writing another book this year?"). The saints at Central Baptist Church are my other family whom I love and serve as pastor. They have encouraged my writing ministry.

Mrs. Gene (Anne) Hendry, always a tactful friend, provided patient proofreading in correcting my errors of spelling and grammar.

Grateful appreciation is due the *Jacksonville* (Texas) *Daily Progress* in whose pages much of this material was first published as my regular column "The Central Idea." Some ideas appeared in *The Pulpit Digest* as "Homiletic Bias," another by-line of several years. Yet other thoughts were printed in *Proclaim* magazine.

Introduction

Heavy is the head that wears the crown. A young king of ancient legend, assuming this awesome responsibility of a new throne, summoned many wise men for his first official act. In his youthful idealism he desperately wanted to avoid the mistakes of previous kings, so he commanded these advisers to collect for him all the world's wisdom.

Twenty years later the leading philosophers, scholars, and holy men of his realm brought him ten thousand heavy volumes. The king was overwhelmed. "I don't have time to read all of that," he said. "Condense this great storehouse of wisdom into fewer volumes."

Ten years later they returned with five thousand books which still discouraged the monarch. "Reduce it to what I can read and remember," he commanded. This process happened again and again.

Finally the king cried, "Time is running out. My eyesight is failing, and my life is fleeting by. Compress what you have written into the smallest possible space."

One year passed and a chief adviser returned to counsel the king, now on his deathbed. "Here it is, your Majesty. We bring to you the bare history of mankind condensed to this one sentence: 'They were born, they suffered, they died.' "

This legend offers a sobering view of reality, but it doesn't present all the facts. So don't leave now. There's more to this story because Jesus, King of kings, brought meaning and purpose to life.

Two thousand years ago our Creator entered human history in the form of the God-man—Jesus Christ. Yes, He was born that first Christmas in a manger. He came, taught, lived, loved, and then died willingly according to a greater plan and purpose. Jesus showed us God. The Lamb of God became our perfect and final sacrifice on the cross. And that's not all.

The devil's dark tomb of death could not hold Him! On that first Easter morning He arose! In that earthshaking demonstration of divine power over death we learn that life does not end in a graveyard. No longer is death "the end." For followers of Christ the most appropriate epitaph reads "to be continued."

From the cradle to the cross, from advent to Easter. These two festivals of faith which we annually celebrate mark the beginning and the climax of our Lord's earthly ministry. No matter how often we tell His story, it's still timely. It never changes from season to season.

Sometimes the preacher's well runs dry, however, in creative illustrations for Christmas, Easter, and other celebrations of the faith. Teachers, speakers, and writers need a different perspective or fresh ideas in presenting these familiar truths. This little volume is sent forth with a prayer that God will use these pages as sparks on dry tinder to fuel the flames of faith.

Part One

From the Cradle

Thoughts, reflections, illustrations, and texts for the Christmas story

An Image of the Invisible

He is the image of the invisible God, the first-born of all creation. For in him all the fulness of God was pleased to dwell (Col. 1:15,19).

In a famous cathedral in Rome a magnificent fresco radiates beauty. Every colorful detail has been painted with patience, but for centuries few visitors to the cathedral actually appreciated this work of art.

Why the absence of appreciation? No one blamed the artist for a lack of mastery or the viewers for lack of manners. Instead, the problem was its location on the inside of a high and lofty cathedral dome.

Everyone trying to look up that high for too long received a stiff neck and eyestrain. Thus, physical discomfort prevented enjoyment and appreciation of this masterpiece.

Finally someone with common sense solved the centuries-old problem. A large mirror was placed just above the floor level. A sight once too distant and difficult to behold was, in effect, brought down to a more human level. Guests can be seated to study and appreciate all the splendor of this superb painting.

That's just what God did for us on that first Christmas. The invisible God came down to us on the human level. Jesus is the image of the invisible God. He is no longer a God way out there in the stars too distant or difficult to behold.

The ancients believed that anyone who actually saw God face to face would die. One ought not seek such familiarity with God. Keep your distance from the Divine! Not even Moses was allowed that favor at his commissioning service when he sought to see God's face. He would see only God's glory (Ex. 33:2).

With the revelation of God through Jesus Christ, that prohibition was reversed. Now we must see God face to face—or we die!

No Longer to Wait

For to you is born this day in the city of David a Savior, who is Christ the Lord (Luke 2:11).

George Washington Carver claimed to be a simple man. Yet the brilliant black scientist took a simple peanut and wrought miracles which were anything but simple.

With God's guidance Carver developed thousands of agricultural and industrial products from the lowly peanut. His goal was helping Southern farmers, many of them black, harvest a profitable crop on their land long since exhausted by cotton. They prospered from Carver's success.

In his later years Carver was invited to Washington, D.C. for a congressional hearing which attracted considerable attention. Everyone was eager to meet the modest miracle man. Influential dignitaries accompanied by reporters met the scheduled train seeking a star.

No one really noticed the gentle soul dressed in his usual ragged suit and dragging a heavy case filled with dramatic experiments ready for congress. He was lost in the crowd.

When Carver asked a redcap for assistance, the fellow looked him over quickly. "I'm sorry, Pops, but I've been sent down here to meet a very important man—a big scientist." Then before Carver could introduce himself the frantic seeker scurried away on his mission.

The modest little saint waited for the welcome committee which never found him. Finally he managed to handle his own luggage, sought his own accommodations in a colored boarding house, and later appeared on schedule before a surprised committee of congress.[1]

Surely our Lord understood. On that first Christmas the expected Christ came almost as unnoticed. God had readied the world in "the fullness of time" for the long-awaited Messiah. Then He arrived. But not as a famous personage. Not with fiery chariots and flaming judgment.

The Savior of the world slipped almost unnoticed into a humble village where His only lodging was a stable among animals. He chose to be born as a babe to a peasant couple. They laid Him in a manger where lowly shepherds briefly worshiped Him before returning to their flocks. So much for His first night on earth.

"What about the foreign kings who followed His star?" you ask. Surely they count as a welcoming committee. Yes, but we aren't certain they were kings. And we know they likely arrived later because the Christ child was by then in a "house" (Matt. 2:11).

The truth is plain. On that first Christmas night a world which claimed to be awaiting the Divine King still missed His appearance. Little has changed since then. Most people still don't realize this great truth. We no longer need to wait for God's appearance. He has already come. That's why the Christmas celebration is so vital in sharing our faith.

Note

1. C. W. Bess, "No Longer to Wait," *Proclaim,* Oct.-Dec. 1978, p. 27.

The Spirit of Christmas Past

Do not be conformed to this world, but be transformed by the renewal of your mind, that you may prove what is the will of God, what is good and acceptable and perfect (Rom. 12:2). Do not lie to one another, seeing that you have . . . put on the new nature, which is being renewed in knowledge after the image of its creator (Col. 3:9-10).

All good things must end, but by the time Christmas finally arrives most of us are too exhausted to care. No other celebration begins so early and lasts so long.

After gifts are given and exchanged, after relatives leave and decorations are packed away, what then? Can Christmas cheer survive the January bills?

After Christmas little Lucy mutters, "Rats! Phooey! Everything is hopeless! Who cares?" Charlie Brown asks "Lucy, what in the world is the matter with you?" Again she shouts, "Rats! Phooey!" The last cartoon shows her walking away only to turn and drop a casual comment to the puzzled Charlie Brown. "Of course you realize that I'm just experiencing my regular, post-Christmas letdown."

Is this the "Spirit of Christmas Past"? When we return after Christmas to the regular routine, we should be changed. The season ought to leave a lasting imprint on our lives like that of the shepherds.

A Christmas tradition in Washington, D.C. is the "Night of Miracles," an annual pageant by the U.S. Army Chorus and Band. One scene pictures the angels inviting four shepherd brothers to worship the Christ child. Who would keep watch over the sheep while they went to Bethlehem? The youngest brother objected because he was frightened to remain alone, but the brothers promised a quick return.

On the way back to the flocks two mischievous shepherds ran ahead to playfully scare their brother. This humorous scene makes a clear point. These two brothers had lost the Christmas spirit already. They were not changed but remained what they were before—immature and shallow jokers.

Then the eldest arrived to comfort his younger brother. With a radiant expression he shared every detail about the Christ child. He had returned to life's routine "glorifying and praising God for all that they had heard and seen" (Luke 2:20).

Now it's your turn to continue Christmas. The only real way to make "the spirit of Christmas past" into a year-round celebration is by a changed life!

The Time Traveler

For the Son of man came to seek and to save the lost (Luke 19:10).
I came that they might have life, and have it more abundantly (John 10:10).

Yes, truth is stranger than fiction. But how often yesterday's fiction actually becomes today's truth.

The space program brought Flash Gordon to life while modern technology has made real those futuristic weapons of space comic strips. That feared death-ray gun is now commonly known as a laser beam.

One comic strip character who has yet to be incarnated is Alley Oop. The caveman who emerged as a comic strip character years ago remains our most popular time traveler—in fiction at least. With Doc Womug at the controls our neighborly Neanderthal regularly travels between ancient Moo and modern America.

The popular *Star Trek* series on television employed a similar miracle of technology in the transporter room aboard the starship *Enterprise.* Captain Kirk and his crew could beam down to distant planets below. They could even lock in on the coordinates of citizens below and beam them up unwillingly.

Will this electronic transfer of warm bodies be the mass transit of tomorrow? In our computer-controlled world, some dreamers believe it's possible. After all, if we can transfer credit, letters, pictures, movies, and even money—why not people?

Once the complex code is cracked for dissolving physical life and reassembling the living cells elsewhere, we could easily move through the "time zones" of history! Or so the dreamers fantasize.

If that sounds farfetched, let's set the record straight. History records that with Jesus it has already happened at Christmas.

A preexistent God (Is there any other kind?) created everything including time which is just another dimension of a created order. God still rules above these created dimensions of time, space, and matter, and He intervenes where necessary to help us come closer to Him. He briefly appeared in the form of angels and often with direct word for His prophets to relay. But the final revelation was in person when God wrapped Himself in human flesh and appeared as a baby.

While Jesus usually traveled by the earthly method of walking, we know He sometimes appeared and disappeared at will. Jesus walked on water. After His resurrection He moved effortlessly through locked doors of an upper room, appearing from place to place.

Why did Jesus become a traveler through time? Not to entertain us or illustrate science fiction come to life. He came for only one purpose —our salvation.

Familiar is Fine

> Have nothing to do with godless and silly myths (1 Tim. 4:7). For the time is coming when people will not endure sound teaching, but having itching ears they will accumulate for themselves teachers to suit their own likings, and turn away from listening to the truth and wander into myths (2 Tim. 4:3-4).

The speaker cleared his voice, looked over the small gathering, and then buried his nose into his notes. This would be another of the many Christmas programs this season, but he would try his best to be original.

"According to an old legend," he began. That introduction hinted something extra was being added to the traditional Christmas story. It's the urge to originate, to be different. Oh well, let's hear him out.

This story is about an unnoticed creature too small and insignificant to be included with the camels, donkey, and sheep. In the excitement of that joy-filled night no one bothered to share the Christmas spirit with him.

If only he could see the infant and offer his gift. But what to give?

Taking a small amount of hay in his mouth, he slowly inched his way toward the manger. It seemed like a journey to forever, but the distance across the stable was magnified due to his small size.

After crossing a distance equal to the oceans, he arrived to offer his contribution to the Christ child. The baby Jesus smiled at him. So thrilled was this tiny donor that he literally glowed.

"And since that time," the speaker concluded, "this creature has been known as the glowworm."

The glowworm? Children giggled while some of the adults raised eyebrows. How shall we respond to sentimental nonsense which actually mocks Scripture and our Savior?

Only one hearer, a child at that, was honest enough to speak up. "I thought we were going to have the real Christmas story. I like it better from the Bible."

Amen! Why try to improve what is already perfect? This timeless story needs no help from myth or imagination. It was fine the first time ever told without fantasy or fairies.

As to the concern that the story is too familiar, what's wrong with that? We don't demand that our best friends change their faces on the grounds that they've become too familiar!

The Advent drama is no shallow story requiring decoration with legends. Study those Christmas characters carefully because all humanity seems represented. There's an evil king, lowly shepherds, mysterious and majestic Wise Men from afar, a noble foster father, and a pure maiden mother.

There's enough grist here for any mill, so let's stick to a faith resting on facts. We need not trifle with this treasure.

The Stargazers

The people who walked in darkness/have seen a great light; those who dwelt in a land of deep darkness,/on them has light shined (Isa. 9:2). When they saw the star, they rejoiced exceedingly with great joy (Matt.

2:10). The true light that enlightens every man was coming into the world (John 1:9).

Beneath a cloudless Arizona sky astronomers trained their telescopes toward the constellation Orion and reported a breathtaking discovery of "the first star born in our time!" At this Tucson observatory Dr. Donald N.B. Hall said: "It's by far the youngest star whose age is clearly identifiable." While conceding that only sensitive instruments can now detect the faint light, he promised that it is drifting our way and will soon become visible to the naked eye on earth.

Ah, that's good news for stargazers! The story made headlines in many major dailies across America.

But wait. You'd best read the details before you rush outside tonight searching for this new star. Astronomers, like geologists, think in epochs, ages, and long periods rather than human life spans.

It seems that our astronomers really had their heads in the clouds on this one. Just when do they anticipate the first natural sighting of their new star by the unaided human eye? When pressed, they agreed on about twenty thousand years from now. That's give or take a few thousand years either way![1]

And that's news? Don't hold your breath waiting to see this new star so far away that it takes fifteen hundred years just for its light to travel to earth.

Time was when only preachers talked about "pie in the sky by and by." Now the astronomers are being misunderstood the same way. Perhaps we've eaten too many instant potatoes and rushed too often to meetings.

Strange that people will get excited about a vague new star twenty thousand years in the future but give little thought to their own judgment ahead. No matter how intriguing the future may sound, somehow they never get around to doing anything about it. While living in the "here and now" they neglect the "by and by."

Historians tell us that the ancients looked for a sign from the heavens. One common hope among peoples of many different cultures was the coming of a God from heaven to rule on earth. The Christmas star invited and then led some distant foreigners directly into this divine drama unfolding at Bethlehem.

Early Christians understood how Jesus fulfilled Gentile hopes as well as Jewish prophecies. Believing that Jesus came to all the world, they changed that world for the better while preparing for His imminent return. Small groups of worshipers met at night and in the pre-dawn hours in that era before Christians earned Sunday as the Lord's Day. Worship began and concluded with a constant watch heavenward toward the stars.

Note

1. *Jacksonville* (Tex.) *Daily Progress,* Dec. 22, 1977, p. 4

Givers Must Receivers Be

He came to his own home, and his own people received him not. But to all who received him, who believed in his name, he gave power to become children of God (John 1:11-12).

Leave it to Charlie Brown and the Peanuts family of cartoon characters to explain the Yuletide season. In their annual television special, Charlie Brown just can't get into the Christmas spirit. Thus his little friend Linus observes: "Charlie Brown, you're the only person I know who can take a wonderful season like Christmas and turn it into a problem!"

What about you? One need not be an Uncle Scrooge to turn Christmas into a problem. It happens to the most loving and generous people when they want to do *all* the giving.

Then what happens when we try to give to them? They say, "Oh, you shouldn't have!" Unfortunately, they really mean it. They want the blessings of giving but not the obligation of receiving. That creates problems at Christmas time.

How easy the virtue of independence becomes the vice of pride. Honestly translated it is the attitude: "I don't need you because I can go it alone. Your giving to me would obligate me and take away my independence."

Study again the manger scene where God gave His greatest gift. He who came to give His life a ransom for many actually began by *receiving.* Christ received gifts from Magi and adoration from shepherds. As an infant He accepted food, clothing, and other physical care lovingly provided by Mary and Joseph.

True. It is "more blessed to give than to receive," but the Bible speaks about receiving and giving. It takes both, and God came to do both. He allowed those participants in the first Christmas pageant to be both givers and receivers. Being gracious as a receiver allows others to share these opposite blessings of giving.

Like most military men in general, and Navy pilots in particular, Captain Howard Rutledge lived a self-sufficient life until his plane was shot down over North Vietnam. In seven terrible years as a prisoner of war under the worst conditions, he learned how to receive with joy life's little blessings. Every breath of air and each moment of life became a gift from God. Perhaps the most profound observation recorded by his book, *In the Presence of Mine Enemies,* describes his food. "When one is dying of starvation a bowl of sewer greens is a gift from God."[1]

Giver or receiver? Jesus showed us how to be both! Receiving is the only route by which we enter heaven and relate to a giving God. Giving is a joy by which we bless others.

Note

1. Howard and Phyllis Rutledge, *In the Presence of Mine Enemies,* (Old Tappan, N.J.: Spire Books, Third Printing, 1977), p. 34.

Love Misunderstood

> For I am sure that neither death, nor life, nor angels, nor principalities, nor things present, nor things to come, nor powers, nor height, nor depth, nor anything else in all creation, will be able to separate us from the love of God in Christ Jesus our Lord (Rom. 8:38-39).

It was one of those days when everything went wrong, time wasted with nothing accomplished. Never mind that the world was celebrating another Christmas season. I was just too busy to care. No "Hail, to the conquering hero!" tonight.

Cancel any welcome-home ceremony. The calendar was clear, and I was going to be home doing nothing. All I wanted was to collapse in an easy chair, bury my head in the evening newspaper, and be left alone.

A sensitive mate like mine understands that mood. Somehow Mary knows just how much time I need before being ready to talk again.

Unfortunately, the youngest member of our family had not yet become sensitive to his father's frustrations and exhaustion. Having waited all day for his dad to come home and play with him, this two-year-old wasn't easily refused.

Mary tried keeping him busy in the kitchen while she warmed the supper which I'd missed. Then the telephone rang and little Craig took advantage of her distraction to get back to me with the same insistence. "Daddy, let's play."

Twice I told him firmly, "Daddy wants to read his paper now. We'll play later. Be a good boy and leave me alone."

The third time I was more direct. Raising my voice and eyeing him sternly, I blurted, "Craig, didn't you hear me?"

There! That should take care of the matter. I resumed my reading until a couple of pages later a faint sobbing came to my attention. Lowering the newspaper I saw a little boy still frozen in his tracks.

Big tears were rolling down his cheeks. When our eyes met and he was sure he had my attention, he asked softly, "Daddy, do you still love me?"

My heart was broken. Somehow in the confusion of life under the same roof a person precious to me had questioned my love. At that moment the Christmas gifts under our tree didn't matter to Craig. He had offered love which was misunderstood.

In the weariness of this old world our best intentions don't always get communicated. Sin does separate. Even God's perfect love gets confused and ignored by a busy world. The sentimental season of the world's first Christmas was no exception.

Shepherds, Wise Men, Simeon, and a few others rejoiced, but a cruel king misunderstood completely the love behind God's appearance in the form of a child. A jealous Herod tried to eliminate any possible rival, even children. In a blind and bloody rage he ordered all little ones recently born in Bethlehem to be put to the sword. God's best was greeted with Herod's worst.

A lesser love would have given up, but not God! He showed us that ultimate love accepts the risk of rejection. The door to God's heart is always open. Even in sorrow, Christmas was not canceled. How can we neglect so great a salvation or misunderstand a love so tender?

Person to Person

> Behold, the name of the Lord comes from far (Isa. 30:27). He who has seen me has seen the Father (John 14:9).

It was my day off and the backyard leaves had to be raked. Already the telephone had interrupted me three times, so when my wife waved for me again I begged off busy. "But it's long distance," she countered. As I hesitated for a moment, she added the clincher: "It's person-to-person."

Well, that's different. Someone really wants me enough to pay a long-distance operator. Calling for me by name stirs my feelings of self-importance. As it turned out the caller was a salesman peddling real estate in Florida. He failed to convince me, but at least he knew how to contact me personally for his presentation.

When an American President wants to contact someone, the world's most persistent team of telephone operators tracks that person down and clears the lines. It doesn't matter what the distance, the cost, or who may have the circuits tied up. "This is the White House operator. Please hang up so this line will be open to the President." All that for a presidential person-to-person call.

Ours is a world of division and distance where continents are separated by great oceans, mountains by valleys, and nations by language. Yet the greatest distance of all is that division between God and man caused by our sin. "But your iniquities have made a separation/between you and your God" (Isa. 59:2).

This great gulf between God and humanity was spanned by something even better than a person-to-person call. God Himself came *in person.*

To some simple shepherds on a nearby hillside, God sent an angelic chorus to announce "good tidings of great joy." With specific instructions where they could find the newborn King now present on earth, they left immediately and found God in the form of an infant wrapped in swaddling clothes.

Later other would-be worshipers arrived in Jerusalem. They had left months before on the same search mission for God by following a star from faraway lands. The shepherds had returned and the holy family had moved into a house, so at least one additional night had elapsed.

Such a remarkable appearance surely drew others, but whose journey was the longest? No doubt about it. God came from the greatest distance that He might be with us *in person.*

The Empty Manger

You will find a babe wrapped in swaddling cloths and lying in a manger (Luke 2:12).

Some years ago a Western city reported a sad situation for the approaching Christmas season. The manger in their city park would be empty.

No, they had not yielded to public pressure from some outraged citizen or organization that was against Jesus. Neither were they under a court-imposed order to empty the cradle of the Christ child. The crisis was of a more common nature.

During the previous Christmas season a thief had removed the central character from their manger scene. It had gone unnoticed until the last day when workmen came to dismantle and pack the display for another year's storage.

The other statues were safe. Mary, Joseph, shepherds, Wise Men, sheep, camels, angels—they were left alone. Only the Christ child was missing.

In announcing their loss the city fathers appealed to the unknown thief. Would he please return the baby Jesus? No questions would be asked, no charges filed.

The incident provoked more than outrage. It became an occasion of city-wide grief. Why would anyone do such a thing? This was unchristian and un-American.

God surely must smile at such shallow grief. How quickly we condemn so brazen a culprit when in truth we all share that guilt.

The central figure of Christmas is so neglected that His disappearance goes unnoticed for days. What's new about that? We generally ignore Him the rest of the year as well.

Which is worse—one common crook who steals His plaster image or millions of casual Christians who ignore His real presence?

The Christmas season reminds us that God cared enough to send the very best. May we care enough about Him to live our very best.

> Take heed lest you forget the Lord your God . . . lest when you have eaten and are full, and have built goodly houses and live in them, and when your herds and flocks multiply, and your silver and gold is multiplied, and all that you have is multiplied, then your heart be lifted up, and you forget the Lord your God (Deut. 8:11-14).

God with Us

> All this took place to fulfill what the Lord had spoken by the prophet: "Behold, a virgin shall conceive and bear a son,/and his name shall be called Emmanuel" (which means, God with us) (Matt. 1:23).

The four-year-old didn't want to stay alone in the dark bedroom. Mommy assured him that he wouldn't be alone. God would be there with him. His childlike reply? "But I want a God that has a face!"

That child speaks for us all. Deep within our souls we long to see God up close. For centuries mankind stood a restless watch under the stars, searching the heavens for some sign of God, longing to see Him face to face. Surely God would come someday.

Have you ever tried to assemble a jigsaw puzzle without a corresponding picture to guide you? Some pieces just naturally fall together, but until a theme or outline gradually emerges, you are left wondering about the final view. That had always been our dilemma before the incarnation of Jesus.

What would God be like? Until we saw Him face to face, it was an impossible puzzle. Human flesh cannot see divine spirit, so God came in person to fit together the final pieces.

"And the Word became flesh and dwelt among us, full of grace and truth; we have beheld his glory, glory as of the only Son from the Father" (John 1:14).

So how big is God? He's big enough to create and rule an unending universe but small enough to fit in the form of a newborn babe. God weighed perhaps seven pounds and six ounces that night, but He was all love and very visible. Is there anything more visible than a baby? It was the only way we creatures of such poor vision could see Him.

During World War Two a child lovingly looked at her father's picture. Longing for his return she asked her mother, "Wouldn't it be wonderful if daddy could just step out of this picture and be home?" That's what God did in Christ. Although the distance was great, He simply stepped out of the stars to be with us.

No longer should people wring their hands and complain, "What's this old world coming to?" The Christmas event boldly proclaims, "Look what came to this old world!"

Christmas Bedlam

Glory to God in the highest, and on earth peace (Luke 2:14, KJV)

It was planned as a worship scene, a living tableau of Bethlehem's manger complete with live animals. Unfortunately, it was too real.

We had no problems with the cow and gentle lambs which played their roles well. Never mind that we couldn't find a camel. After all, we reasoned, the Wise Men would have parked their camels out back.

But the goats? We now know from sad experience that this creature doesn't belong in a manger scene. Our Lord was right on target when He described judgment as separating the sheep from the goats.

What did the goat do, you wonder? We could forgive everything except his nibbling the costume of the third Wise Man. The other Magi could have handled that, but not the frightened female wrapped inside that old bathrobe and terry cloth turban.

No, we weren't campaigning for women's lib. Our third Wise Man just wasn't wise enough. He was studying for a final exam (Too bad, but he flunked anyway!). The girl was the only stand-in available.

Anyway, she screamed and the goat jumped. Then it kicked. Down came the back wall. Out went the lights. Away went the goat.

The virgin Mary tried to ignore it all, but the goat was her borrowed responsibility. She wasn't about to pay cold cash for a gone goat. See Mary run.

That did it! Our Bethlehem had degenerated into bedlam. What had begun with the best of intentions became the worst of Christmas confusion. But that's nothing new. "Bedlam" describes how we celebrate Christmas today.

The word goes back to the 1400s when a fine London hospital named St. Mary of Bethlehem opened its doors to the insane. Perhaps the hospital seemed less religious than before. It was certainly more noisy.

For some reason people dropped St. Mary from the name. Then they eventually contracted and corrupted the last part. Bethlehem became Bethlem and finally bedlam, a place of noise and confusion.

Now the personal question. How do *you* celebrate Christmas in your life and home?

Do we need noisy parties, a crowded calendar of events, and confusion around the Christmas tree? That first manger scene was simple and not put-on. The celebration of Bethlehem's greatest birth need not become bedlam. Worship ought not cause confusion but peace. "For God is not a God of confusion but of peace" (1 Cor. 14:33).

We Are Never Too Old

> And let us not grow weary in well-doing, for in due season we shall reap, if we do not lose heart. So then, as we have opportunity, let us do good to all men (Gal. 6:9-10).

For millions of us around the world, Christmas would be incomplete without the music of George Frederick Handel. His *Messiah* with its "Hallelujah Chorus" is among the most-loved music scores ever. The German-born composer will always be remembered and appreciated.

But it was not always so. In fact, Handel found success very elusive. Everyone recognized his ability, but somehow his big break never came.

Once in London Handel composed a magnificent oratorio which should have established him as a great composer. He invested his life savings in its production with a full orchestra. But then on opening night a bitter snowstorm ruined attendance. Again Handel went broke and faced a debtor's prison.

Those were his darkest days. Critics claimed that England's music tastes were changing. Handel was considered to be burned-out, old and outdated, a "has been" who never was. He would have been forgotten except for one final opportunity.

Late in life he was asked by Charles Jennens, a wealthy friend and writer, to compose music and orchestration for an oratorio on the biblical theme of redemption. Jennens had compiled the text completely from Scripture.

At first Handel estimated the task would take a year, but the challenge so captured his imagination that he worked day and night. The project was completed with 260 pages of manuscript in only twenty-four days!

It was a phenomenal physical feat, but the spiritual impact was just as great. Hearts were stirred. The old man had fought back from failure to make his greatest contribution to the world's music.

One wonders how many other great gifts to the world are lost because we give up too soon. We may once be too young, but we are never too old. Whether nine or ninety, the world waits for us to make it a better place for living.

Now look closer at the Christmas story. Receiving the infant were saints of many years and great age who had not grown weary in well-doing. The devout Simeon and patient, prayerful Anna remind us that we are never too old!

How to Feel Better

> He who sows bountifully will also reap bountifully. Each one must do as he has made up his mind, not reluctantly or under compulsion, for God loves a cheerful giver (2 Cor. 9:6-7).

Did you hear the one about a traveling salesman whose illness was reported in a medical journal? No joke! It really happened.

This medical oddity was described in the *Journal of the American Medical Association.* Dr. Elman G. Lutz finally diagnosed the patient's unusual case of compression sciatica.

Don't let the medical talk throw you. Simply stated, the patient suffered a persistent pain in his left side. You probably know the feeling.

He tried all the doctors. No one, from orthopedic surgeons to practical chiropractors, provided any relief.

Even the famous Dr. Lutz had given up. The patient might as well slip back into his street clothes—end of examination.

But wait! By chance the good doctor bumped into his patient in the hallway as the poor sufferer was leaving with his noticeable limp.

The doctor called the salesman back. "What are you going to do today?"

"Same as always. I'm getting into my car and driving several hundred miles on my route."

"Just like that? If you sit on that fat billfold all day long, that's your problem!"[1]

Case solved! A simple "walletectomy" (removal of the wallet) healed the man.

Do you suffer from some similar problems? Perhaps it's not your back but your heart that bothers you. Try this cure. Empty your wallet for a higher cause and you will feel better—if not in the sciatica, at least in the spirit. Give till it helps your hurt. Givers feel better!

In no other season is this spiritual satisfaction more obvious. The Wise Men gave gifts of gold, frankincense, and myrrh. Although fondly remembered by tradition as three kings, it is far more likely that these outsiders were more modest in their means. Wise men sensitive in the ways of God are seldom rich!

They invested much in a long journey and appropriate gifts for the newborn king. "I will not offer burnt offerings to the Lord my God which cost me nothing," King David insisted (2 Sam. 24:24). Surely those seekers by way of the star knew how to give in the same spirit of sacrifice.

Note

1. *Church Chimes,* First Baptist Church, Shreveport, La., May 2, 1981.

Part Two

To the Cross

Thoughts, reflections, illustrations, and texts for the Easter season

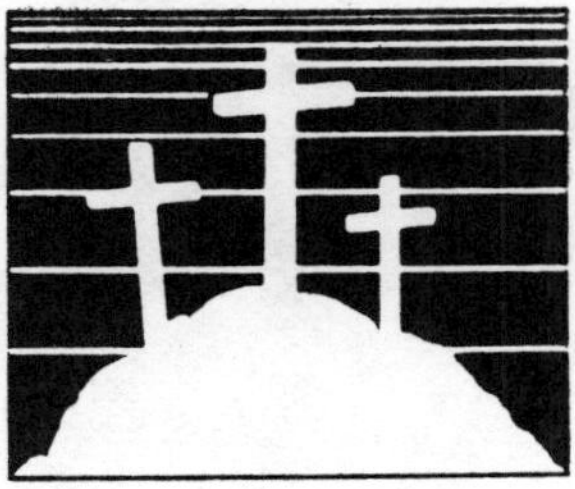

Come Alive!

But whoever drinks of the water that I shall give him will never thirst; that water that I shall give him will become in him a spring of water welling up to eternal life (John 4:14).

How do you tell thirsty people in other lands about your product? Some good ideas just don't translate very well. Consider the case with a popular soft drink when they chose an advertising theme "Come alive with ______." It was a success in America but not elsewhere.

The soft drink company placed an advertisement in the Taiwanese edition of *Reader's Digest.* The artwork was fine but the "Come Alive" theme needed translation into the Chinese characters. Just before publication an alert Chinese editor caught the mistake. The Chinese version read, "______ brings your ancestors back from the dead."

The same theme did not fare as well in a German translation which actually ran in print for several weeks. Germans were mystified by a dramatic claim: "Come Alive Out of the Grave."[1]

In case you're interested, it really is possible to "Come alive out of the grave." But not with any earthly drink.

God's Word promises continued life through our faith in Jesus Christ. How can we be sure? Because Jesus Himself suffered death, went to the grave, and returned alive! Later the disciples remembered how often Jesus had used this illustration of satisfying the human thirst for eternal life.

To the Samaritan woman at Jacob's well, our Lord offered living water. She should have understood sooner when He discussed that favorite theme of Old Testament prophets. Jeremiah had claimed God's people "have forsaken the Lord,/the fountain of living water" (17:13). Zechariah talked about those same living waters (14:8).

No doubt about it. Jesus is the only source of living water which satisfies our ultimate thirst for real life. Had He not come alive out of that grave, His claims would have been forgotten. But the often-married Samaritan woman at the well finally understood. Now it's possible for us to really come alive!

Note

1. *Jacksonville* (Tex.) *Daily Progress,* Nov. 10, 1978, p. 3.

Hardhearted

> For me to live is Christ, and to die is gain. I am hard pressed between the two. My desire is to depart and be with Christ, for that is far better (Phil. 1:21,23).

Jeremy Bentham was so impressed by University College Hospital in London that he left his entire estate to the institution. Then the eccentric philosopher sat through ninety-two years of perfect but negative attendance at the hospital's board meetings.

He didn't mean to be so negative. Yet after 1832 he never made a motion or voted in favor of anything.

Bentham's philosophy was generally forgotten, but no one ever ignored his presence. The Englishman remained cold and hardhearted as a body can be.

Not that his body was all bad. For a man born over one hundred years earlier, Jeremy Bentham was remarkably well preserved with the best-embalmed body money could buy.

No wonder he sat silently through all those board meetings. He was stone dead and present in body only.

In accepting the dead man's considerable estate, the hospital had followed to the letter some strange instructions. Bentham's corpse was preserved in a seated position, attired in a nice suit and hat, and enclosed in a mahogany case with glass doors. There he reposed in a chair with his firm right hand on a favorite walking stick.

Insane? Perhaps. But Bentham's logic was consistent with his refusal to believe in a soul or any form of life outside the body. It was important to Bentham that his body be kept safe because he had no options for life outside the body. He was really a practical sort of fellow who thought he had found the ideal caretaker for his body in an attempt to survive longer.[1]

What a pity! Anyone who lives in body only has a limited life indeed. To dismiss any possibility of life beyond death is a negative and ultimately costly philosophy.

We Christians are more secure in a faith which does not fear what death can do to the body. "And do not fear those who kill the body but cannot kill the soul; rather fear him who can destroy both soul and body in hell" (Matt. 10:28).

Because Jesus gives us power to rise again after physical death, we can see the good in final release from a temporary shell meant to serve us only during this brief sojourn on earth. Death is not the end of life but only of the physical body.

> For we know that if the earthly tent we live in is destroyed, we have a building from God, a house not made with hands, eternal in the heavens. So we are always of good courage; we know that while we are at home in the body we are away from the Lord, for we walk by faith, not by sight (2 Cor. 5:1,6-7).

In those few words Paul described our situation. The body cannot be in two places at the same time, nor can it stay here on earth forever. The only logical solution for believers, then, is to accept our limitations as an invitation to life eternal in the very presence of God. "We are of good courage, and we would rather be away from the body and at home with the Lord" (2 v. 8).

Note

1. David Wallechinsky, *The Book of Lists* (New York: Bantam Books, 1978), p. 450.

No Neutral News

> Do not be afraid; for I know that you seek Jesus who was crucified. He is not here; for he has risen, as he said. Come, see the place where he lay. Then go quickly and tell his disciples that he is risen from the dead (Matt. 28:5-7).

As part of his carefully cultivated image, John Chancellor worries about his eyebrows. Seriously. He wants neutral eyebrows.

The television network commentator works hard to appear impartial on television. According to his standard of "professional neutrality," a newsman ought not betray feelings through biased words or voice tone. The goal is total objectivity which neither agrees nor disagrees with events being reported.

But what do eyebrows have to do with neutrality? Chancellor practices in front of a mirror to rid himself of eyebrow power—the last place on his face which might reveal feelings of doubt or condescension![1]

And what does that have to do with the cross and resurrection reports? Just this. We don't find any neutral observers in early accounts of a dead Jesus coming back to life.

Take Mark's version. First to arrive at the open tomb were women described as "amazed" and "trembling." They were "[astonished]" and "afraid" (see Mark 16:6-8).

The resurrection was anything but ordinary news to be reported by disinterested observers. Either it was history's greatest hoax—or God had indeed come back from the grave! You either believed or you disbelieved. No one was left unmoved.

A leading Pharisee named Saul reacted with such anger at the event that he tried to kill everyone who dared believe. Then the living Jesus challenged him on the Damascus road. And Saul believed too! Saul moved into the Gentile world as Paul, the missionary with a message about Jesus being alive.

In *every* case the people who heard this Jesus story responded passionately one way or the other. Even in Athens, where philosophical ideas were entertained with the nearest thing the ancient world knew about professional objectivity, Paul got results. Some "mocked," others wanted to "hear [him] again," while still others "believed" (Acts 17:32-34).

How we've changed. Nobody these days wants to make choices or take a stand in the spiritual realm of life and death. People are curious but not committed. We are like an open-minded newscaster who claims to be above the news and beyond personal involvement.

By that standard the ostrich is most objective with his head stuck in the sand! We are two of those three famous monkeys who pretend to hear no evil and see no evil. Are we to close our eyes in moral and spiritual matters?

Some events demand our response. If a neighbor is being mugged in your front yard, you are already involved. If someone telephones that your house is on fire, will you be disinterested?

Suppose on a vacation cruise your captain orders, "Abandon ship!" Will you consider yourself a neutral observer while your fellow passengers enter lifeboats?

A blind refusal to respond can lead to disasterous consequences. We Christians have passionate feelings about both the cross and the empty tomb. We're involved in a matter of life and death, and we believe!

Note

1. *The Wall Street Journal,* Mar. 30, 1982, p. 24.

Voices from Beyond

> If the Spirit of him who raised Jesus from the dead dwells in you, he who raised Christ Jesus from the dead will give life to your mortal bodies also through his Spirit which dwells in you (Rom. 8:11).

No escape artist ever rivaled Harry Houdini who laughed at locks, straitjackets, iron boxes, and heavy chains. During a well-publicized career the famous magician successfully escaped from every device cunning men brought to him.

After the death of his beloved mother, Houdini became obsessed with communication beyond the grave. He exposed many frauds and promised that if anyone could indeed speak from the spirit world, he would find a way.

Always one to prepare every detail in advance, Houdini developed an elaborate code known only by his wife. Then he died suddenly on Halloween of 1926.

His wife waited in vain and finally gave up. The secret code died with her, yet on every anniversary devoted followers still assemble at Houdini's grave. They've heard nothing from beyond.

Perhaps Houdini died too soon. A California engineer now promises modern technology can do this trick. The "impossible" is accomplished at the simple push of a button on a $10,000 electronic tombstone operated by solar energy.

Stanley Zelazny claims his invention can play up to ninety minutes of personal (prerecorded) testimony. The Plexiglas-enclosed, solar collector is maintenance free, works even in snowstorms, and last indefinitely.

The thirty-seven-year-old inventor believes that rock stars, politicians and other ego-conscious humans will make him rich. "It's going to change the course of the world," he says. "America and the world wants this."[1]

While not exactly a voice from beyond, this gab from the grave does make interesting conversation. After all, aren't we all curious about the other side of death?

Yet there's a better way to hear from the beyond without having to trust fake mediums or resorting to technological gimmicks. Jesus has already gone through that dark door of death, left His light for us, then returned to tell about it. His is the only report we can believe as a voice from beyond.

The best part is His promise that we who truly believe in Him have no need to return from the grave. While our bodies turn to dust for the duration of this age, our lives continue in heaven with Him. "Even though I walk through [not just into a dead end valley but all the way through!] the valley of the shadow of death,/I fear no evil./I shall dwell in the house of the Lord for ever" (Ps. 23:4,6).

Note

1. *Jacksonville* (Tex.) *Daily Progress,* Jan. 29, 1981, p. 3.

The Sting

Death is swallowed up in victory.
O death, where is thy victory?
O death, where is thy sting?
The sting of death is sin . . . But thanks be to God, who gives us the victory through our Lord Jesus Christ (1 Cor. 15:55-57).

We don't hear many horror stories about killer bees these days. For a while the scare headlines had us worried when an African strain of bees escaped from a laboratory in South America and started moving north. Animals or people disturbing their nests were attacked with such fury that many died.

Fortunately, the vicious bees mellowed when they gradually interbred with docile strains of domestic bees. Our cooler climate in North America also deterred them. Best of all, you can relax with the assurance that bee stings are seldom fatal anyway, that is, unless you are highly allergic to insect venom. Then it could be a sting of death.

A father was driving his child to school when a bumblebee flew into the car. Because the boy had once nearly died from a bee sting, he became hysterical. The quick-thinking father caught the bee in midair with his free hand and tossed it out the window. Then he pulled over to calm the boy.

His son refused to be comforted. Now he was desperately afraid that his father would die. "Oh, no," the father replied, showing his hand which was only slightly swollen. "The sting won't hurt me like it would you, so I took the sting for you."

That's what Jesus Christ did for all people. By God's perfect standard we who sin deserve death. That means all of us. Because we are indeed guilty, our fear of death is real. The sting is sharp and sure but not final. Victory belongs not to Satan but to the Savior who died in our place. Jesus paid the price for us. Now death has no victory over us.

Note

1. *Jacksonville* (Tex.) *Daily Progress,* Jan. 29, 1981, p. 3.

A Giant Scam

To them he presented himself alive after his passion by many proofs, appearing to them during forty days, and speaking of the kingdom of God (Acts 1:3).

In 1869 the world's most famous farm was in Cardiff, N.Y. Workmen digging a well there had discovered the body of a fossilized man over ten feet tall and weighing nearly three thousand pounds. Owner William Newell looked happy.

What a discovery! Two professors from Yale, one a paleontologist and the other a chemist, agreed that the giant was authentic. So did poet Ralph Waldo Emerson and Judge Oliver Wendell Holmes.

Other experts smelled a hoax, but that didn't hurt ticket sales. The controversy helped Newell raise prices from five cents a visit to one dollar. P.T. Barnum, the circus showman and master of deception, offered to buy the act. Somehow Newell seemed to be expecting him.

Intense negotiations followed, but Newell was overconfident. He spurned Barnum's offer of sixty thousand dollars for a three-month lease of the "fossil."

Barnum stomped off. "He'll be back with a better offer," Newell boasted. But the slick showman went out and hired himself a smart sculptor. Next year the curious no longer needed to journey way out to the country. They paid higher prices to see a "twin fossil" when Barnum's exhibit came to their towns.

Having lost his best prospect, Newell sold to other investors. This group lost heavily and sought an injunction against Barnum.

Surprise! The showman admitted his giant wasn't real. He was only promoting a copy of the original and gladly explained everything. A block of gypsum, a stonecutter with chisel, sulfuric acid to age the creature and lo—a duplicate! No law against that!

The public caught on. The original was probably a hoax, too. An investigation revealed that Newell had a silent partner, George Hull, who had once purchased a great block of gypsum in Indiana and had employed a Chicago stonecutter.

Pressured by mounting evidence, Hull confessed. Angry investors then sued Newell. The only money anyone made was by Barnum, probably the original target of Newell's scam.

Newell and Hull learned too late. Never try to con a con artist. Never play the other person's game.

In the wilderness temptations Satan tried to convince Jesus to take a shortcut on His earthly mission. "Avoid the pain and rejection of people. Make a deal with me and you won't need suffer the agony of a crucifixion or darkness of death. You only need to bow down and worship me."

It would have been the ultimate hoax, the greatest rip-off. But our Savior wanted nothing to do with Satan's scam.

Check the facts. Jesus went willingly to the cross. He endured death. Then He arose. Proof is there for anyone with an open mind. Our Lord's resurrection was real.

Surprise at Sunrise

> And the diviners see lies; the dreamers tell false dreams, and give empty consolation (Zech. 10:2).
>
> And as Jesus was going up to Jerusalem, he took the twelve disciples aside, and on the way he said to them, "Behold, we are going up to Jerusalem and the Son of man will be delivered to the chief priests and scribes, and they will condemn him to death, and deliver him to the Gentiles to be mocked and scourged and crucified, and he will be raised on the third day" (Matt. 20:17-19).

In 1970 Alvin Toffler introduced "future shock" with an intriguing look ahead. His best-selling book by that name made Toffler our most popular prophet since H.G. Wells.

What kind of prophet? Not the biblical brand or the fortune-teller type with a crystal ball. The new breed, preferring the title futurists, base their predictions on progress and statistical probabilities. Their expertise is technical and scientific. Or so they say.

These futurists promise us a leisure-filled life made possible by strange new inventions if we prepare ourselves for a radical restructuring of society. Traditional forms of family, marriage, church, and society will have to be changed forever. Those unable to adjust will suffer future shock.

Surprise! Future shock has turned into future shuck. While the world changes with new inventions, we still have the same old problems. I believe Toffler struck out like all the others.

This century began with H.G. Wells in his prime as a fiction writer. He was amazingly accurate as a prophet of technological progress. But not always.

In 1902 the first submarine was successfully launched. Even children realized that this age-old dream of mankind sailing under the seas had become established fact, but Wells disagreed. "I must confess my imagination refuses to see any sort of submarine doing anything but suffocating its crew and floundering at sea."[1]

And consider this recent example. In 1956 the Astronomer Royal of England publicly scoffed about the possibility of interplanetary rockets. He said that space travel "is utter bilge" and that man would never make it to the moon. In only thirteen years our American astronauts proved him wrong.[2]

How could these brilliant men be so wrong? They were logical. People base their opinions on the latest word from science but without all the facts. While science may offer the latest word, it's never the last word.

Two thousand years ago they nailed Jesus to a cross. The Roman executioners were professionals in that business and they knew how to kill. Never had a condemned victim escaped death.

Then they buried the body in a tomb, rolled a heavy stone in place, secured it with a Roman seal, and posted a Roman guard. That did it! Jesus was forever dead with not even a rumor of life possible.

Why the extra precautions? Jesus had predicted His death and resurrection, although no one took Him seriously—not even His disciples who fled in fear.

All the combined wisdom of the world had decreed this one inescapable fact. "When you are dead, you are dead."

Just the same, the Romans took no chances. The local religious authorities who had arranged this crucifixion to rid themselves of Jesus were nervous and wanted assurance.

So be it. The corpse would not move. There was absolutely no possibility of even hope for life. Death is final.

Then came sunrise on that first Easter morning. Surprise! Jesus is alive! Someday we'll learn that the only promises and predictions worth believing are those from God.

Notes

1. David Wallechinsky, *The Book of Predictions* (New York: William Morrow and Co., 1980), p. 398.
2. Chris Morgan and David Langford, *Facts and Fallacies* (New York: St. Martin Press, 1981), p. 133.

The Convincing Cross

> For the word of the cross is folly to those who are perishing, but to us who are being saved it is the power of God (1 Cor. 1:18).

The Canadian prospector recognized the small mound as a grave—obviously that of an Indian child. Wilderness had almost reclaimed the clearing near a peaceful lake. It was a sacred scene.

A tiny picket fence encircled the pile of rocks on which a rusty lunch box rested. Curious, but with reverence, he opened it. Inside were the child's toys left behind for the possibility of a next life.

A tin whistle, green crayon, and plastic animals from a candy box are somewhat shallow preparations for eternity. Knowing this, those parents included gifts for the great Indian spirit. One petroleum jelly jar held a single tea bag and another had tobacco with six matches.

The grave was an eloquent testimony to parental love. They were just poor Indian trappers who did everything their custom demanded. But before they left their child, they did one thing more—just in case. As a tribute to the white world's God, they erected a cross.

The cross. Sometimes a sign of superstition, often misunderstood, but forever a symbol of hope.

Just as a compass always points north, Christian hope always points toward the cross. There Christ died as a perfect sacrifice for all mankind.

Oh, death and graves seem so final. But not with Jesus Christ! He arose! His resurrection on that first Easter morn proves His ability to save and keep safe even beyond the grave.

If only those Indian parents could have known the God who requires no gifts on graves. Instead, He gives us the gift of eternal life which we must accept only before death.

The cross symbolizes not just death and darkness but dawn and deliverance. Through Christ it's the convincing cross.

Note

1. Len Shannon, "Burial Customs of Other Cultures," *The American Cemetery*, Nov., 1970, pp. 22-23.

Blessing from Blunders

> We know that in everything God works for good with those who love him, who are called according to his purpose (Rom. 8:28). And I, when I am lifted up from the earth, will draw all men to myself (John 12:32).

There is a well-known brand of soap that has two uncommon qualities. It's known as "the soap which floats" and is the oldest of the best-sellers. But it wasn't always that way.

Years ago this soap was just another brand among many. Then a factory foreman blundered by leaving a batch of new soap unwatched in the cooking vat during noon hour. His lunch was delayed and the soap overcooked.

Rather than report the mistake and run the risk of dismissal, the foreman decided to make the best of it. He shipped out this new batch anyway. It seemed to clean just as well—although now much lighter.

The results surprised everyone. Rather than complaints the company was deluged with orders for this floating soap. The foreman was not fired but promoted when he cooperated with company chemists to revise and modify the old formula for "the soap that floats."

Blessing sometimes come from blunders and a silver lining is often behind a dark cloud. Good can come from grief and profit from peril. Pick up the pieces, be positive, move on. It's often possible to make something better out of something bad.

That's the way God works with us. We don't often do right the first time, but He's always ready to salvage the situation no matter how bad we make it.

The cross is the great example. That bitter instrument of agonizing death represented the ultimate rejection. Men feared the cross and turned their faces away. So degrading was this cruel torture that Roman citizens, even those guilty of the worse offenses, were guaranteed a more honorable execution.

Jesus didn't deserve that kind of death, yet "for the joy that was set before him endured the cross" (Heb. 12:2) and changed our thoughts about death. His shame and suffering offered eloquent testimony of a sacrificial love by the sinless Lamb of God.

No longer would the cross represent defeat. Jesus took the greatest blunder of mankind and turned it into something better. "For the word of the cross is folly to those who are perishing, but to us who are being saved it is the power of God" (1 Cor. 1:18).

After Easter

I was in the Spirit on the Lord's day (Rev. 1:10).

Auguste Comte, a French philosopher and skeptic, was teasing the

English writer, Thomas Carlyle, about his faith in Jesus Christ. Comte declared he could begin a new religion to replace Christianity.

"Very good," replied Carlyle. "All you need do is to be crucified, rise again the third day and get the world to believe you are still alive. Then your new religion just *might* have a chance."

The resurrection is a hard act to follow! And so is Easter when Christians pack the pews to celebrate that event.

People who seldom tip their hats to God any other time observe this holiday by dressing in their newest spring clothing and attending church. They don't expect to hear some great celebrity preach that day. Everyone knows that even an ordinary local pastor can draw a crowd on Easter.

But after Easter? One pastor concluded that his own preaching must be the greatest in the world. His members crowded in each Easter and in thirty minutes received enough of his wisdom to carry them right on through another full year!

How far we have drifted from the early Christian tradition. Church historians say that the ancient world had new moons and regular feast events, but not weekly holy days. Only the Jews had a sabbath every seven days.

Christianity was first nurtured in the cradle of Jewish religion, but Jesus so fulfilled the Old Testament law that early believers made a dramatic break from the past. They moved their worship to Sunday.

Why worship on Sunday, the first day, rather than Saturday, the last day of the week? Something dramatic happened on a Sunday. A dead Jesus was raised alive from the dark tomb!

That first generation of Christians needed no regular rite of spring such as Easter. They couldn't wait that long. Rather than an annual holiday they made resurrection Sunday a weekly celebration.

The Saturday sabbath was no longer their day. Sunday is now and forever the Lord's Day.

Which brings us back to our original question. What can we do for an Easter encore? Simple. Go back to church every Sunday.

Rabbits and Resurrection

. . . that I might know him and the power of his resurrection (Phil. 3:10).

For fun and profit no other city has been so successful in identifying with a religious celebration. New Orleans *is* the Mardi Gras celebration. Tourists from everywhere overflow the city for parades and dances beginning two weeks before Mardi Gras Day, a legal holiday for the locals. The free-spending visitors are so welcome that the festival is said to be an annual savior of their economy.

These festivities originated with an ancient Roman custom of drunken feasts before a brief fast. It's a very human response. If I'm going to diet, then I might as well have a good time of it the last few days before the ax falls.

Nothing but a major emergency could cancel Mardi Gras in New Orleans which has endured through invasions and several wars with only one interruption. That happened in 1979 when leaders of a militant union for policemen called a strike. Without police for crowd control most of the parades were canceled. A few moved to the suburbs.

When it appeared that the strike would not soon be settled, one radical union leader hung a dead rabbit outside police headquarters. He shouted defiantly, "You can tell them Easter is dead now, too."

The news media had a field day with that threat. Really now! The symbolism just doesn't fit. There's no way a rabbit can symbolize Easter. This Easter bunny business goes too far. The furry little creature may be cute to cuddle, but rabbits can never point to a risen Christ because they have no resurrection power.

The cross is a better symbol. Once hated and feared by subservient peoples as an instrument of torture and execution, the cross became a powerful symbol for victorious Christians no longer afraid of death's darkness.

The open tomb is another good symbol. Unlike other graves which receive a body for ultimate decay, this was a temporary tomb needed only until Sunday morning when Jesus was raised from the dead.

The Lord's Day is yet another symbol, a weekly reminder that Jesus can change worship from the Jewish sabbath to the first day of the week for a Christian Sunday. Even our calendar offers a testimony of history when we divide time by BC (before Christ) and AD (anno Domini, in the year of the Lord.)

We have symbols and reminders enough that rabbits are not necessary for Easter. It's time we Christians stop cooperating with a world which perverts our holiest celebrations. The resurrection power of Jesus is enough.

The War Is Over!

> Comfort, comfort my people, says your God./Speak tenderly to Jerusalem, and cry to her/that her warfare is ended, that her iniquity is pardoned (Isa. 40:1-2).

Remember how World War II ended? Not with a whimper but a bang! Fighting in the Pacific theater concluded suddenly amid the rubble of two atomic blasts which shook the entire world.

Yet thousands of Japanese soldiers missed the news. Entire garrisons were isolated when American forces simply bypassed island fortresses on the way to Japan. Because their commanders could not envision the possibility of peace, they had fled to hills and caves under orders to die for the emperor or fight forever. Later the governments of America and Japan sent messengers into those areas with good news. "Come on out! The war is over!"

Starving soldiers slowly stumbled from caves and hideouts in final surrender, although some stayed. In 1974 Lieutenant Hiroo Onada, the last known survivor, emerged from the jungle after thirty years and was captured by local citizens. Why had he not given up earlier when it was obvious that Japan had lost the war?

Lieutenant Onada tried to explain that he had not been trained to surrender in shame, nor had he received any orders to do so. Therefore, the soldier continued the status quo, which was war.

Are others still in the jungle fighting a war long since settled? Many think so. Three former soldiers recently traveled to the Philippines seeking a friend missing thirty-four years. Solid evidence has convinced them that their sergeant is still on the run from the Allies and unaware that the war is over.

We Americans cannot understand why anyone would continue a useless effort in a war long after it has been settled. Why fight alone with only defeat ahead? Better to surrender now, make peace, and enjoy a new and better life which defeat brought the Japanese.

No doubt God has the same thoughts about us. It's the same paradox of all people the world over. By insisting on our own selfish ways, we have rebelled against the Creator. That spiritual problem has caused war, misery, hurt, and death as our common lot.

But two thousand years ago God settled it all through the death of Christ. Somehow that death reconciles us with God. We were defeated, but yet we win. The gospel message carried to all is "Come on out. The war is over!" We can have peace with God.

How to Die

> I am the resurrection and the life; he that believes in me, though he die, yet shall he live (John 11:26).

No subject is more fascinating. We will lean closer and listen intently to hear the last words of a dying soul.

In drama the death scene cannot be rivaled for impact. Dying quotes make lively literature in everything from ancient classics to modern best-sellers.

But real life is more awkward for the listener who is asked for help. What can you say to that dying person before he steps from earth into eternity?

Joe L. Ingram of Oklahoma tells about an Anglican clergyman during the First World War. Like all loyal countrymen, he was volunteering for service with his nation's military.

The minister sought a chaplain's position with the British army. Bishop William Taylor-Smith, chaplain general of the British Army, received his application.

Taking a pocket watch from his vest, the chaplain general held it thoughtfully and said: "I am a dying soldier on the battlefield with three minutes to live. What do you have to say to me?"

The minister was confused and could not respond. "Now I have only two minutes to live. What can you tell me to help my soul?" Again no response.

Finally the minister fumbled for his Book of Common Prayer, but the general stopped him. "That will not be enough at a time like this."[1]

Yes, even men of the cloth stammer in the presence of death. It is never easy to find the right words for the dying.

Not that we are without schools, seminars, workshops, and how-to books to learn about life. But no one teaches us how to die. And no wonder. Until we've traveled to the other side, we cannot comfort others from our own personal experience. Yet we are not left in the dark.

Only one individual in history has tasted death's final sting and lived to tell about it. And you can be sure that Jesus Christ was dead. Those Roman executioners practiced their deadly craft with professional skill. Never had a condemned prisoner survived a Roman execution.

But a dead Jesus rose alive from the grave! Death's cold grip could not hold Him, the grave could not contain Him. Those simple words He first spoke to His disciples have since become the comfort needed by the dying. "I am the resurrection and the life; he that believes in me, though he die, yet shall he live" (John 11:26).

Note

1. *Baptist Messenger,* Oklahoma City, Ok., Aug. 18, 1983, p. 10.

Lovesick

> But God shows his love for us in that while we were yet sinners Christ died for us (Rom. 5:8).

Six months after the death of his wife, Thomas A. Edison began looking for a new mate. The practical-minded man would leave no stones unturned in a systematic search reflecting his scientific nature.

Although he liked to be portrayed in the media as a genius who worked in solitude, Edison had quietly assembled a fine research team. These capable men greatly multiplied his effectiveness without detracting from his glory.

For this personal project Edison sought the help of friends in nearby Boston. He would apply the same principle of letting others do preliminary fact gathering.

Edison hated social events, but dinner parties in the home of Boston friends helped him meet many candidates at one time. He was proud of this efficient approach.

So what happened? Rather than making a calm, rational choice, the thirty-eight-year-old inventor fell head over heels for an eighteen-year-old lass from Ohio.

She was everything he wasn't—religious, cultured, and beautiful. Plus young enough to be his daughter!

Edison threw his normal caution to the wind. Until Mina Miller would agree to marriage, he played the lovesick fool with outrageous behavior more typical of a teenager.

An iron-willed, self-disciplined workaholic found himself bitten by the love bug. He was unable to concentrate in his research lab and whiled away weeks writing silly notes to an eighteen-year-old.

Fortunately, the future of American industry was brightened when this lovely young lady finally consented. Edison soon settled back down into his inventive rut.

Funny thing about Mina Miller. She wasn't bothered by Edison's poor hearing or even his chronic halitosis. She brushed the dandruff off his coat and fell in love with him.

That is one aspect of love which sees the best in others. Mina totally accepted Edison because love is not always practical or rational.

We mortals do strange things when in love. And so does God. He loved us even while we were sinners unaware of His life-giving sacrifice through Jesus on a cross.

"But God shows his love for us in that while we were yet sinners Christ died for us" (Rom. 5:8).

Part Three

And Other Celebrations

Thoughts, reflections, illustrations, and texts for national holidays, special Sundays, and daily living

1
Celebrations of National Holidays

New Year's Day

Happy New Year

The word of the Lord came unto me a second time (Jer. 1:13).

The highly paid experts of our American advertising industry certainly understand the impact of key words. Can you guess their favorite word used most often in those slick ads or on the colorful boxes or bottles designed to catch a shopper's attention?

No, it's not *Sale!* The single most powerful term in sales and advertising is spelled with only three letters—*New!*

We are always willing to try something new. Even the most basic and familiar brands of soaps or foods periodically boost sales with that simple word. Every product on the store shelves seems to be "new and improved."

How many times will advertisers challenge manufacturers to change a successful product? Never mind. Most often "new" refers to the package or quantity rather than product change.

A familiar greeting in this season is "Happy New Year!" There's that word again. The "happy" part is elusive enough, but can anything in life really be new? The obvious reason so many unhappy people stay that way year after year is a lack of positive change to make life better. They keep the same old attitudes and habits guaranteed to continue their unhappiness for another round of familiar failures and lost opportunities. The new year brings nothing new for them because they change little in life beyond the calendar on the wall.

Louise Fletcher Tarkington described the old year as a shabby old coat to be dropped at the door of a new year and never worn again. Her poem was entitled "The Land of Beginning Again." That's an intriguing thought. If only we could move to a land where failures are forgotten and everyone receives a second chance each new year.

It's possible! We need not move to some distant land to begin again. The Bible openly describes people who failed through sin or lack of faith but then received a second chance from God to start over.

God chose Moses to deliver Joseph's descendants out of Egyptian slavery, but Moses could not wait. In an impulsive act of anger, he murdered one of Pharaoh's foremen who was beating one of his Hebrew brothers. By his own hand Moses had pushed aside forty years of privileged preparation.

The man with a guilty conscience ran away and hid himself in the land of Midian. We who have read all the story want to warn Moses about wasting another forty years as a hired shepherd tending his father-in-law's sheep. He just didn't seem to understand that God was ready with forgiveness and a second chance. An entire generation died in Egyptian slavery while waiting for Moses to accept God's offer to start over.

King David had once desperately needed that new beginning. Like Moses, this former shepherd was destined to lead a nation to greatness. And he did. Then one spring David stayed home at the palace while his armies went forth to fight his battles. David committed adultery with Bathsheba, then murdered her noble and heroic husband in a futile cover-up. The king deserved death but received a second chance when he wept and prayed his way back into God's favor to become a man after God's own heart!

Elijah savored God's greatest triumph on Mount Carmel but then lost heart and fled in fear before the threats of a defeated but still wicked Jezebel. God finally convinced the prophet to accept another mission. Elijah started over and then never looked back.

It's the gospel of the second chance, the opportunity here on earth to start again. With God we can turn our back on past failures, "forgetting what lies behind and straining forward to what lies ahead" (Phil. 3:13).

But when? Not last year but now. The new year offers a timely pause to look ahead at life as a book of 365 pages. Each page represents a day in your life for the coming year. This record shall be your testimony forever written in secret thoughts, good intentions, and especially deeds. What will it say about you?

You shudder at that idea, but the urge to know the future overcomes your fear. So you open the book titled *My Life Next Year.* Inside you find every page blank!

The book is not yet written. You hold the pen of a daily diary of life to be filled in one day at a time. Your future is not yet determined. The new year waits before you clear, uncluttered with failures, and open to wonderful possibilities of change. Now is your chance to change and make it a better year with God's help. Happy New Year!

New Year's Day

Perfection

> But one thing I do, forgetting what lies behind and straining forward to what lies ahead, I press on toward the goal (Phil. 3:13).

In the British Museum in London rests the final draft of Thomas Gray's masterpiece, "Elegy Written in a Country Churchyard." Lovers of English literature marvel how every word seems so carefully chosen. And they were.

Gray wasn't satisfied with his first draft, so he rewrote it. Then he improved the poem a third time. He continued for eight years.

With all that persistent polishing, however, Gray never considered his poem complete. In the museum display we can see each successive copy carefully penned by hand. All seventy-five drafts!

Are you a perfectionist like that? If so, your goals in life keep climbing higher and higher. What you wanted to accomplish last year is not good enough now for this new year.

That is fine, up to a point. We should press on for improvement so our future will improve over our past.

But not unto perfection. That is an impossible goal here on earth. Eventually every project and every person must stop short somewhere.

Doing our best is only half the task. Then we need wisdom to stop worrying about what we might have done further.

Many high achievers are like Thomas Gray. They are never satisfied with themselves and keep pushing to produce more.

Efficiency experts advise us to do the job well. Take time to evaluate and improve. Then move on, leaving both success and failure behind.

Good advice. But hardly new. The apostle Paul had that forward look for a successful future. He wasn't preoccupied with past failures (and he had many of those!) but pressed on ahead. That's a good formula for a happy new year.

Valentine's Day

Tablemate

Do not be mismated with unbelievers (2 Cor. 6:14).

He was already a living legend. No man was reputed to have made more money or eaten more food than millionaire salesman "Diamond Jim" Brady.

She was equally successful on stage and in song. The buxom actress Lillian Russell also enjoyed food in prodigious quantity.

Together they made a perfect pair in highly publicized dinner dates. In that gilded age of the Gay Nineties, no couple attracted more attention when frequenting Manhattan's finest restaurants.

The Brady-Russell duo could deplete the complete food stock of small, cozy establishments. Twelve-course meals were common.

Could they share a future around food? New York's most eligible bachelor thought so. He decided to propose marriage to his ideal tablemate.

The genial Brady, also known as "Gentleman Jim," considered how to impress Miss Russell. He had long believed in friendship, fortune, and food.

Those three interests were shared by both. That's why "Diamond Jim" left his diamonds home on that fateful night and brought cold cash instead.

In dramatic fashion Brady dumped one million dollars into her lap. Would Miss Russell agree to permanently join him for a table team of two?

Russell graciously declined the offer believing that marriage might ruin a beautiful friendship. The two remained friends.

Until then no one had ever rejected the charmingly colorful businessman. Women the world over questioned the sanity of this famous singer.[1]

Yet it was still a wise decision. Money does not make a marriage. A life-sharing love cannot be bought in the marketplace.

Today's marriages often involve legal agreements describing property settlements in event of divorce. These contracts are signed *before* the marriage ceremony as a necessary precaution because "love is blind."

Whatever happened to character? And commitment? Rather than seeking a cash-and-carry arrangement for marriage, consider integrity, honesty, and self-respect. At least Miss Russell understood that marriage deserves more than a tablemate or money mate.

Serious Christians go further to insist that husband and wife are soul mates. The Bible presents marriage as an ideal relationship to be found only in God's will and based upon an equally shared faith in

Jesus as Savior. Only when both partners are committed to Christ can love be truly blind.

Note

1. Irving Wallace, *The Book of Lists, No. 2* (New York: William Morrow and Co., 1980), p. 271.

Mother's Day

Equality

For there is no distinction between Jew and Greek; the same Lord is Lord of all and bestows his riches upon all who call upon him (Rom. 10:12).

Equality. That's an American belief based upon the Bible and expressed most clearly in our Declaration of Independence. "All men are created equal."

The American Constitution picks up the theme to go beyond the simple act of proclaiming equality. In the plainest language possible this highest law of our land commands each branch of our government to practice it.

With favoritism and special treatment forbidden, we should expect our national capital to be the very center of equality. Worldly-wise politicians know better.

Where is the best example of equality to be found? No doubt about this one. Look no further than the mother of more than one child. Mothers have that natural instinct to love and treat each of their children fairly.

During General Eisenhower's presidency a reporter asked the

"First Mother" for an interview about her son. She answered, "Which son? I have three sons, you know."

A wise mother loves equally each of her children while still recognizing individual success. That kind of mother's love can also keep us humble, however, as another great general learned.

After Napoleon Bonaparte conquered all of Europe and had consolidated his power, he proclaimed himself emperor. The Little General loved playing that role. He even revived the custom of loyal subjects kissing the hand of royalty.

Everyone went along with the new emperor. Staff officers, former nobles, and even high officials in the church obeyed. But not his mother, Letizia. Once when she greeted him in a crowd, he extended his hand for the formal courtesy. She slapped his royal knuckles aside! In a loud voice his mother reminded him that he was still but one of her eight children!

Let's hear it for mother. She's the only person on earth who can divide her love among many children and still give each child all her love.

Ever wonder who first taught mothers that trick? Don't look around. Look up. God is the Originator, the Top Teacher in all virtues who loves us all. Equally. Impartially. Totally. He doesn't play favorites. We're all equal.

Mother's Day

Thanks, Mom!

Her children rise up and call her blessed (Prov. 31:28).

Her three children promised a special Mother's Day, beginning with breakfast in bed. No, she must not help, although from the noise Mother wondered if some assistance were really needed.

In the kitchen the children brought out three pots, two frying pans, a double-boiler, three mixing bowls, a chopping board, six measuring spoons, and eight serving dishes. Mom was delighted. She said it was the best gelatin she had ever tasted!

For children Mother's Day is a good occasion to learn how to say "Thanks, Mom." Sometimes mothers are the last persons to hear that word even though they offer us the first human relationship here on earth. All that we become later in life begins first in this wonderful relationship.

The ministry of Moses cannot be explained until one realizes the influence of his mother during those early, formative years. Moses had been officially adopted by Pharoah's daughter and was being raised and educated in the courts of Egyptian royalty. Years later, however, he identified with God's people and shared their reproach rather than enjoy the pleasures of sin for a season. Without a doubt Moses had been greatly influenced by his paid nurse who was in reality his own mother.

Behind the greatness of Samuel stood a devout mother named Hannah. She had long prayed for a child as a gift from the Lord and had promised even before his birth to give him back into God's service. While Samuel was still a young child, she brought him to the Temple where he then lived in full-time training for God's service.

Thus has it always been. Mother is the first teacher and greatest influence on children. She deserves her day.

A London editor sought an interview with Winston Churchill concerning the many teachers who had influenced the great statesman. Unable to secure a personal appointment with Churchill, he did preliminary research on his own. Then he mailed this list of names asking Churchill to write some brief comments about any of these teachers he remembered. Later he received the list back from Churchill blank. The only comment was: "You have omitted to mention the greatest of my teachers—my mother!"

Father's Day

Forgotten Father

A child's glory is his father (Prov. 17:6, TLB).

Kenneth Chafin, a Southern Seminary professor who preaches and writes often about stronger families and better fathers, arrived home barely in time for the evening meal. He was in a hurry and preoccupied with his thoughts for a speaking engagement that night.

His five-year-old daughter had her own plans for father. "Daddy, will you stay home with me tonight?"

Her plea pierced his soul. How could he tell her? Chafin felt guilty knowing his assigned subject for a group was "What a Good Father Ought to Be."

It was too late to cancel. To soften her disappointment and help her feel important, he asked her help in his speech. Could she describe what she thought it meant to be a good daddy? During the hurried meal he jotted her ideas down on paper:

1. Catch a fish
2. Build a fire
3. Fly a kite
4. Catch a butterfly
5. Plant a flower
6. Get a kitty cat out of the mud

Then Chafin folded the paper and drove to the meeting. Only as he was waiting on the platform to be introduced did it suddenly hit him.

Nothing that his daughter wanted in an ideal father required money. What she wanted was a little time with her father.[1]

Fathers don't all earn the same amount of money, so what they give to their children in the way of worldly things varies widely. Yet all fathers have the same twenty-four hours each calendar day. Their responsibility to share time with children is the same.

Beyond the basics of food and shelter, what a child needs most is a little time with dad. Other gifts can be lavished upon children until they are spoiled rotten, but a father has given nothing of value to his children until he gives himself.

A father who neglects his children in this matter will be the forgotten father of tomorrow. Better for both that he invest some time wisely in his own flesh and blood.

Note

1. Kenneth Chafin, *Help! I'm a Layman* (Waco, Tex.: Word Books, Second Printing, 1972), p. 79.

Father's Day

The Best Crop

Lo, children are an heritage from the Lord (Ps. 127:3, KJV).

Train up a child in the way he should go, and when he is old he will not depart from it (Prov. 22:6).

Until recently, many fathers in America farmed. By their standards, success could be measured by the bushel, the bucket, or the barrel.

One dirt-poor farmer never achieved a bumper crop, partly because he could not afford good land and a strong mule. A little shack betrayed the family's modest means. Yet, they were happy, even in poverty.

The father worked hard and taught his only son the satisfaction of honest toil. They labored, laughed, and loved together as a family, but to the boy it seemed that they mostly labored. Every day was full of chores.

Once a neighbor dropped by for a brief visit when father and son were chopping weeds in a field of waist-high corn. This prosperous friend knew how to raise corn.

He casually commented, "Your corn is tall enough that these weeds won't hurt. There's no need for you and your boy to work so hard chopping them."

The poor farmer wiped his brow and replied: "Maybe. But I'm not just growing corn. I'm raising a boy."

Smart dad. His son could have been given free time for lazy days and idle thoughts. Instead, father and son kept busy together.

Later the son graduated from high school as valedictorian. His father was excited. His own son would give the traditional speech to class and community.

During that speech, the uneducated father wept openly. He whispered to his wife: "That boy is the best crop we ever raised. Yes Momma, the very best crop we ever raised!"

He is a wise father who knows how to raise children. Unlike a corn crop, we don't always have another year to better raise a child.

Perhaps we need more fathers who teach their children how to labor, laugh, and love together. As the twig is bent, so grows the tree.

Independence Day

Chosen for His Own

Blessed is the nation whose God is the Lord; and the people whom he hath chosen for his own inheritance (Ps. 33:12, KJV).

What could be more exciting than teaching English all summer with a good friend at Hong Kong Baptist University? But even the most rewarding jobs sooner or later settle into a routine.

The shock of a strange culture plus heat and humidity left us exhausted. We were ready for any kind of break when a typhoon slowly moved into the city, which began closing down. Suddenly we became happy thinking about a couple of days off.

We stood on the roof of our mission compound watching the scurry of those seeking safety. It didn't seem particularly dangerous to us. Just a typhoon. Later we moved downstairs to lounge on the bed, stare at the ceiling, and relax.

But not for long. The wind which we had laughed at a few moments before increased in strength and caused the building to shake. Instinctively, we rolled out of bed as thick, storm-proof windows shattered. The pillows and sheets were shredded by glass slivers.

Oh, then we began rejoicing for the right reasons! Not that we had a day off to enjoy, but that we were alive to enjoy it. We rejoiced in the Lord! He had chosen us to live.

On Independence Day we rejoice in a similar mood. God has chosen our nation to live, so we pause for both joy and reflection. We are happy for better reasons than a long weekend off from work with picnics and parades. America is surely a chosen nation.

Who would have dreamed it possible in 1776? A scattered and otherwise insignificant group of thirteen impoverished colonies boldly declared their freedom over oppression. A great experiment in democracy became America's gift to the world. We take credit although it was accomplished long before anyone of us was even born.

A wealthy traveler once passed through a small English town on Sunday and couldn't find a tavern open. He complained, "Why can't a fellow get something to drink in this wretched town?" They could only answer, "Because a man named John Wesley passed this way a hundred years ago!"

Make that two hundred years ago. The names were Patrick Henry, Nathan Hale, George Washington, and John Hancock, but the God was our same Father in heaven who blesses nations when even a small remnant remain faithful to Him.

Go back to the *Mayflower,* that frail, little vessel destined for a new and unknown world. There you see some fathers of this nation preparing to land at Plymouth. They came not as world conquerors, seekers of gold, or even soldiers of fortune and adventure. They came as Christians. Aboard ship they knelt and prayed for God's guidance according to their written vows in the Mayflower Compact:

> "We whose names are underwritten . . . having undertaken for the glory of God and the advancement of the Christian faith, . . . to plant the first colony in the northern parts of Virginia."

God's hand is in our history! When we wonder how we can be so fortunate as to live free in a world ruled and ruined by dictators, Communists, and kings, then we remember our heritage! We begin with God. "Blessed is the nation whose God is the Lord, the people whom he has chosen as his heritage!" (Ps. 33:12).

Note

1. Samuel Eliot Morison, ed., *Of Plymouth Plantation* (New York: Alfred A. Knopf, 1952), p. 76.

Independence Day

Free to Be Dependent

> Live as free men, yet without using your freedom as a pretext for evil; but live as servants of God (1 Pet. 2:16).

Can we ever push a good thing like independence too far? An airline boasted of having the first, totally automated airplane needing no pilot or crew. It was advertised as a "Freedom Flight" and scheduled for an Independence Day departure. The symbolism was not even subtle. Technology would free people from dependence on other people.

The pioneer passengers took their seats and were treated with smooth sailing at forty thousand feet. For those willing to serve themselves, abundant food and beverages were available. After all, everyone was to be independent.

With their destination near they made ready for the historic arrival. A recorded announcement made the routine reminder about fastening seat belts and concluded: "Congratulations again on being the first to fly with independence! Following this recording our automated switching system will lock into a perfect, pre-programmed landing. Don't be afraid for nothing can go wrong, go wrong, go wrong . . ."

Mr. Murphy has a law even for that bit of fiction. If anything can go wrong, it will!

In this case, most of us prefer a real live pilot, a person who possesses skill and training. We gladly submit to the authority of a human pilot who can safely get us to our destinations. Pilots are nice people to have aboard an airplane.

A stirring book and movie came out of World War II—*God Is My Copilot.* What an inspiring thought! As Christians, can we say that God is our copilot in life? Absolutely not! That's the wrong order. God is more than a second-in-command without authority or major tasks until we ask Him to take over so we can relax a minute. He is the captain of the ship.

W.E. Henley went too far in his poem "Invictus."

> Out of the night that covers me,
> Black as the Pit from pole to pole,
> I thank whatever gods may be
> For my unconquerable soul.
>
> It matters not how strait the gate,
> How charged which punishments the scroll,
> I am the master of my fate:
> I am the captain of my soul.[1]

Freedom is fraught with the dangers of trying to be too independent even from God. We want to go it alone, to make our own decisions. Is this not why we were given freedom? Wrong again! We are given freedom by God not to leave but to stay by choice. He does not imprison us to keep us loyal.

A boy boasted to a wise man about a new pet. Inside his tightly clutched hand was a beautiful bird he had trained for special songs. "Whose bird is it?" the philosopher asked. "Well, it's mine, of course," came the reply. "Then why do you clutch is so tightly as if you fear an escape? Open your hands so the bird can have its freedom to fly. If the pet disappears, it was never yours in the first place. If, however, it returns to you, then it is truly yours."

In our case there is no question of ownership. "You are not your own; you were bought with a price" (1 Cor. 6:19-20). Furthermore, we can never truly be independent from God the Creator and Sustainer of the universe. Ultimately, God is just as necessary as food, water, and air. We are far more dependent than independent.

Yet the gift of freedom is still ours that we might choose the measure and depth of our devotion unto God. We are free to choose not how much we can live without God but rather how much we can live with Him.

Perhaps we need another national holiday to follow July Fourth. After we celebrate political independence we could set aside another day to acknowledge spiritual Dependence Day.

Note

1. William Ernest Henley, "Invictus" in *Masterpieces of Religious Verse,* James Dalton Morrison, ed. (New York: Harper and Brothers Publishers, 1948), p. 575.

Labor Day

God's Good Gift of Labor

So whether you eat or drink, or whatever you do, do all to the glory of God. Therefore, my beloved brethren, be steadfast, immovable,

> always abounding in the work of the Lord, knowing that in the Lord your labor is not in vain (1 Cor. 10:31; 15:58).

In a Minneapolis cemetery long known by local residents as the "working man's garden" is a fourteen-foot-high granite monument with this inscription: "This garden has been created in honor of labor—the first lesson mankind had to learn; the foundation of all wealth, all industry, all the arts; great giver of health, sound sleep, and of the most honest dignity that this world knows."

Can you "amen" that? The Bible teaches that labor is a good gift of God. "In the beginning God created . . ." The first verb in the first verse is a working verb. God created or made the world. The creation account concludes: "And God saw everything that he had made, and behold, it was very good" (Gen. 1:31).

Thus the world's first example of work is offered by God. "It was very good." Let's nail down this truth. Work is good.

Like a fine craftsman God stepped back to admire His own work. He liked it. Surely you have experienced this satisfaction, that good feeling of a job well done. You come home "bone tired" from an honest day's toil. Or as a homemaker you stayed and worked yourself weary in cooking and cleaning. Yet you've been productive and accomplished something. It is a good feeling because work is good.

Where do we get the idea that work is a curse? Not from God. When man sinned, God never pronounced a curse on labor. Read it again. "And the Lord God took the man and put him into the garden of Eden to till it and keep it" (Gen. 2:15). That was the work assignment before Adam and Eve rebelled. It was a great job—no problem but pure joy.

Then through sin, man caused the garden and the world to change. "Cursed is the ground because of you" (Gen. 3:17). Adam and Eve were cast out of the garden to scratch a living from soil now dominated by thorns and thistles.

Henceforth the ground would be worked "In the sweat of your face" (Gen. 3:19). Pollution, flood, and fires would now complicate what had been a problem-free task. The ground had been cursed.

But labor was not cursed. It remained a blessing, not a burden; a comfort, not a conflict. Work is still God's gift of accomplishment and satisfaction for all people. Carlyle stated it well: "Blessed is he who has found his work;/let him ask no other blessedness."[1]

Stand outside the plant gate as shift workers leave with bent backs and greasy hands. They can walk proudly even when their faces are covered with grime because, as Thomas Dekker observed: "Honest labour bears a lovely face."[2]

Notes

1. Thomas Carlyle, *Past and Present,* quoted in *Bartlett's Familiar Quotations* (Boston: Little, Brown and Co., 1980), p. 474.
2. Thomas Dekker, *Patient Grissell,* quoted in *Bartlett's Familiar Quotations* (Boston: Little, Brown and Co., 1980), p. 251.

Labor Day

Silver Threads

> For we hear that some of you are living in idleness, mere busybodies, not doing any work. Now such persons we command and exhort in the Lord Jesus Christ to do their work in quietness and to earn their own living (2 Thess. 3:11-12).

Poverty was a very real and unsentimental situation to a struggling musician named Hart Pease Danks. Times were tough in the early 1870s, but at least Danks and his wife met their problems together.

Then came prosperity and fame! The obscure dreamer composed the music to a sentimental song paying tribute to his wife. "Silver Threads Among the Gold" swept the nation, selling over a million copies of sheet music in record-setting time.

For the first time in their lives, the couple didn't worry about last month's leftover bills or the uncertainty of next week's job. They were independent. Whatever they saw and desired, they bought with cash.

Then came the tragedy so typical of "easy money." Bitter quarrels developed between husband and wife over their new wealth. Only a year later Danks divorced the woman immortalized in his ballad.

Ironically, the wealth that magnified their problems soon disappeared. Although "Silver Threads" went on to earn a special niche in musical history, Danks realized no further profit. He had been so eager (some called it greed) for the fast buck that he had sold all future rights for immediate cash, which was soon squandered.

Danks was plunged back into obscurity. Years later he was found in a Philadelphia rooming house having died alone on his knees. Beside him was a faded copy of the still-popular song on which he had scribbled this sad truth: "It is hard to grow old alone."

Here is the supreme paradox of people on the road to prosperity. The final destination of financial independence seldom proves as satisfying as the earlier journey, especially when fortune comes too soon and too easy. Something happens when these hard-driving moneymakers reach their goals. They finally glance in the rearview mirror of the past and wonder why they sped by without enjoying their work.

Like those other blessings of good health and happiness, we never completely appreciate the value of work and vocation until we miss them. In this respect a laid-off machinist shares a dilemma with a jackpot winner too rich to work.

In their book entitled *Suddenly Rich,* journalists Rena and Jerry LeBlanc describe the lives of lottery winners years later. In almost every case the suddenly rich winner had severe adjustment problems. Some lived in fear of kidnapping. All found themselves avoiding people because of the incessant requests for loans from family or friends. Panhandlers and con artists dogged their steps. A majority of these now wealthy people claimed the creature comforts were not worth the happiness they left behind!

Thomas A. Edison made and spent several fortunes while still a young man. He decided that work was more fun than wealth. In later years his wife worried that he worked too much and deserved a vacation. After months of prodding he finally agreed to her suggestion. He would enjoy himself. But where?

Mrs. Edison wasn't about to make a suggestion. That would have to be his decision. "Just decide where you would rather be than anywhere else on earth, and go there."

"Very well," he replied, "I will go tomorrow." The next morning he faithfully kept his promise. He went back to work in his laboratory!

Halloween

Ghost Hotel

For God hath not given us the spirit of fear; but of power, and of love, and of a sound mind (2 Tim. 1:7, KJV).

Explorers, cavalry scouts, and frontier lawmen may have won the West, but a mild-mannered inventor unleased the real force which tamed a wild country. Meet Oliver Fisher Winchester.

While not a violent man, his rapid-fire rifle drove fear into the hearts of all Indians. The awesome weapon spit fiery bullets with repeat efficiency. Outgunned tribes accustomed to Stone Age weapons were doomed.

After Winchester's death his widow worried about the departed spirits of all those Indians. How would they greet her husband on the "other side?"

At first Mrs. Winchester worried only for her husband's soul. Soon she feared what might happen to her dead husband's fortune and to her own soul.

Then she made her greatest mistake. Instead of taking her worries to a God who cares and comforts, Sarah Winchester consulted mediums of the spirit world. From then on it was Halloween every night.

Call them fortune-tellers, psychics, or just plain fakes—but they confirmed her fears. Yes, her fortune was cursed by human and even animal spirits slain by the popular rifle.

What should she do? The most persuasive of her spirit advisers suggested (or demanded) that she placate the ghosts while she had time yet in this world. Make them comfortable. Provide a place where the nicer spirits could dwell. She would need their friendship later.

So began the ceaseless construction of the world's craziest house. Sarah Winchester hired twenty-two carpenters who expanded an eighteen-room mansion into a ghost hotel with 160 rooms spread over six acres!

After each night's seance the energetic widow met her workmen with strange sketches and new ideas. There was never a master plan or any semblance of continuity.

Dozens of balconies and weird windows wound up decorating outside walls. Strange staircases led nowhere.

Because ghosts are reputed to use chimneys rather than doors, forty-seven such routes were provided. The spirits supposedly needed these exits at the bewitching hour of midnight when they regularly returned to the "other side."

For thirty-eight years Sarah squandered a vast fortune on this project of lunacy. Construction finally ceased in 1922 at her death.

Today the Winchester Mystery House stands as mute testimony to the misguided intentions of a woman who feared the false and superstitious spirits of death. How tragic!

Any practical-minded person must lament the foolishness of money so wasted. But far worse was her misplaced faith driven by a misguided fear.

Christians know better. The most desired spot in eternity is not a ghost hotel on earth but a prepared place in heaven. It is not a place of fear or fake spirits. Darkness is forever banished where Jesus will take us.

Good from Bad

We know that in everything God works for good with those who love him, who are called according to his purpose (Rom. 8:28).

Coffee County, Alabama, was a misnomer from the beginning. They grew cotton, not coffee. Although the soil had long been exhausted by King Cotton, local farmers still stayed with the same crop. They knew nothing better.

George Washington Carver, the great black scientist and Christian, tried to persuade farmers to plant peanuts. The legume was ideally suited for that climate and grows well in Southern soil. As an added blessing the plant actually enriches fields long since exhausted by cotton.

Habits of a lifetime are not easily changed, especially when strong, economic forces are absent. Those few farmers who tried peanuts found Carver to be correct, but soon the market was glutted with peanuts. Why grow something you couldn't sell?

Carver's now famous responses led directly to God. He prayed to know everything about the lowly peanut, and God gradually opened unto him hundreds of ideas. Entire industries rose from Carver's research, including cooking oil, peanut butter, soaps, paints, plastics, and fertilizers.

Soon the industries were clamoring for more peanuts. Market price offered sufficient incentives for profit, but it turned out that cotton still held the hearts of poverty-stricken farmers who preferred old ways. Carver despaired of ever breaking the grip of King Cotton.

But then disaster struck. The boll weevil invaded. Because cotton could no longer be profitably grown, the farmers *had* to switch. The results were so spectacular and profitable that a grateful people decided to erect a monument to commemorate this great lesson.

It was inscribed: "In profound appreciation of the boll weevil, and of what it has done as the herald of prosperity, this monument is erected by the citizens of Enterprise, Coffee County, Alabama."

That's a lesson to remember. Often bitter winds of adversity help more than hurt. What seemed disaster brought by boll weevils became a door to opportunity. Good grew out of what was first perceived as bad—gratitude from grief. With God all things can work together for good.

No matter how bad the situation, we can give thanks to God because He can make good from it. "In every thing give thanks: for this is the will of God in Christ Jesus concerning you" (1 Thess. 5:18, KJV).

Thanksgiving

Gratitude

> But thanks be to God, who gives us the victory through our Lord Jesus Christ. (1 Cor. 15:57)

It was a stormy autumn night in 1860 with the waters of Lake Michigan churning up rough waves. Edward Spencer was walking along the shoreline and saw the tragedy happen.

A crowded steamboat, the *Lady Elgin,* was rammed by a freighter loaded with lumber. Within minutes 393 passengers were thrashing in the water as the steamboat broke up and sank a mile offshore.

The nearest help was the small village of Winnetka, Illinois. Very few boats would be available, so Spencer plunged in and swam toward the survivors. In seventeen desperate trips he managed to save seventeen persons. Even then 279 others died.

The young man was acclaimed as a national hero, but he never recovered from the emotional shock of seeing so many die. Unable to resume his studies at Northwestern University, he was admitted to an asylum. He kept asking, "Did I do my best?"

A few years later Spencer, by then an invalid confined to a wheelchair, was contacted by the editor of a Chicago newspaper. The alert journalist had uncovered some old files of the original story and wondered about a follow-up on the now-forgotten hero.

A reporter was sent to interview Spencer on his birthday. What was his most vivid memory of that fateful night?

Spencer sadly replied that *not one of the seventeen persons he had saved ever returned to thank him!*

Gratitude. It's neglected by too many Christians busy for God's glory but forgetful in this earthly grace.

Ten lepers approached Jesus with their tales of woe and pleas for healing. They were tired of being outcasts and separated from society. Their hopes were high when Jesus sent them to be examined by the priests who had medical authority to pronounce them clean if they were indeed healed. But the trip would have to be an exercise of faith in trusting Jesus to work a miracle after they left Him. While they stood yet in His presence, no change was evident in their bodies. Nevertheless, in faith they left on a momentous mission and discovered happily their miracle of healing along the way.

Nine lepers rejoiced and proceeded on their journey. Only one "turned back, praising God with a loud voice." Only one thanked Jesus, and he was a Samaritan. The foreigner whose religious training was considered second-class to that of God's chosen people gave a first-class demonstration of gratitude (Luke 17:11-19).

The fact that he returned alone without the other nine was not lost on Jesus. More in sadness than in anger our Lord asked, "Were not ten cleansed? Where are the nine?"

One out of ten is not a good response rate. Neither is zero out of seventeen, as in Spencer's tragic case. Where are the others? Where are we?

As a national holiday Thanksgiving rolls around with precise, annual regularity. It's time to stop complaining, to pause, and to count our blessings. For one day a year we practice the grace of gratitude.

Here is a better idea. We could designate one annual event on our national agenda to complain, grumble, and close our eyes on all blessings from God and people. Then the other 364 days we could live as a thankful people of God "always and for everything giving thanks in the name of our Lord Jesus Christ to God the Father" (Eph. 5:20).

Thanksgiving

Golden Windows

Take heed lest you forget the Lord your God . . . when you have eaten and are full, and have built goodly houses and live in them (Deut. 8:11-12).

Presnell Wood tells about a boy growing up in a simple cottage nestled on the side of a mountain. Although his family was poor, they enjoyed a millionaire's view of a wooded valley.

Across the valley was another mountainside with a house much more beautiful than his own. With each passing year the boy found it more difficult to be grateful for his own house because this other house had golden windows. With dawn's first light he daily looked out his own window in awe at that beautiful sight. He promised himself that someday he would leave his own ordinary house. His first visit would be across the valley and up the mountain to examine this house of golden windows.

Finally the day arrived for the journey. He left his own house behind and walked steadily all day. By midday he had crossed the valley. It was late afternoon when he approached his dream destination. Yet something was wrong.

Instead of a house with golden windows he discovered a cottage more ordinary than his own. Surely he had made a mistake.

Seeing a little girl playing in the yard of this ordinary house, he asked her, "Do you know where I can find the house of golden windows?"

"Indeed I do!" She pointed back across the same valley which he had traveled to a house on a mountainside. Its windows at that moment were ablaze with the golden glory of a setting sun being reflected off glass.

For a long time the lad stood awestruck. How could it be? Slowly the truth dawned upon him. That was his house! All along he had lived in a house of golden windows.[1]

And so do we all. That's what Thanksgiving Day is all about. On this the most uniquely American of all our holidays, we gather around tables heavily laden with food to count our blessings.

We remember that original Thanksgiving celebration as a golden era, a time of peace and prosperity. This popular image of our Pilgrim fathers feasting upon a cornucopia of American abundance is more legend than truth, however.

It had been a devastating first year for that tiny band. Having come to build a new life of freedom and prosperity, they had encountered the worst of weather, disease, and Indian raids. Over half the colony had perished before spring, but they buried their dead secretly so their desperate plight would not be obvious to enemies.

Somehow the survivors had endured the cruel winter. They had prayerfully planted gardens in small plots painstakingly carved from the wilderness.

Finally came the harvest. It was meager by today's standards, but those men and women of faith gave God the glory. Then they enjoyed a light meal of wild turkey, fish, and corn. Although supplies were still tight, it seemed like a feast.

We associate this season with turkey, but our forefathers thought about corn. For generations American families laid five golden grains of corn beside each Thanksgiving plate as a reminder. Once they had been thankful for a daily ration of only five grains of corn. Then they lifted their hearts in praise and gratitude for God's blessings.

If emotions can be represented by colors, then gratitude is truly golden. We need not travel across valleys and climb mountains seeking someone else's blessings.

Note

1. *The Baptist Standard,* Dallas, Tex., Nov. 24, 1982, p. 6

Thanksgiving

Thanksgiving Anytime

> At midnight I will rise to give thanks unto thee because of thy righteous judgments (Ps. 119:62, KJV).

If you are still searching for the perfect time to be most thankful, then the psalmist offered a suggestion of midnight. In the darkness of life's night, long before dawn, gratitude can be a redeeming grace. Or so Reverend Martin Rinkhart believed when he wrote our most popular Thanksgiving hymn.

Was his beautiful hymn written to commemorate a bountiful harvest during a peaceful period of prosperity? No, it was the worst of times in Europe from 1618 to 1648—"The Thirty Years War."

Rinkhart and his congregation suffered the full force of war's savagery. Their little village in Germany was invaded and sacked three times with almost everything of value destroyed. Half the villagers died.

Faced with that awesome scene of death and destruction, Rinkhart sought God's strength. How could defeated and discouraged Christians live in that kind of world? He fell to his knees in deep, searching prayer.

When he rose the burdened minister sensed a strange answer from God. Nothing had really changed. They could still praise the Almighty with a thankful spirit!

God's presence and power were so vivid in his hurt that Rinkhart expressed his feelings on paper. Then he composed a tune and shared it with his few members. It spread. Even when translated into other tongues, the hymn, "Now Thank We All Our God" expresses a truth which cannot be limited to language. While not written for our American observance of the November holiday, this hymn expresses profoundly our deepest feelings of gratitude. That's because genuine thanksgiving is the universal experience of worship and always appropriate no matter what the season or the circumstance.It can never be limited by either calendar or calamity.

> In every thing give thanks: for this is the will of God in Christ Jesus concerning you (1 Thess. 5:18, KJV).

2

Celebrations of Special Sundays

Youth Sunday

Do It Yourself

So each one of us shall give account of himself to God (Rom. 14:12).

"Lucky Lindy Lands!" That news flashing around the world made Charles A. Lindberg a national hero of past generations. He was the first to fly solo across the Atlantic.

It had been a dangerous mission. "Suicide," the experts had predicted. The frail little plane couldn't carry enough fuel for such a long trip. Lindberg calculated otherwise. A flight plan of pinpoint accuracy would deliver him in France with about a gallon to spare.

But could he stay awake during the monotony of that long flight? It would take all the strength of his youth.

Would the weather cooperate? With few navigational aids he depended upon visual sightings of stars. What happened if the stars were hidden by clouds? There are few landmarks over the open seas. Any slight drift off course would be deadly without fuel and no place to land.

Through all those dangers Charles Lindberg persevered. As he stepped from the plane at Orly Airfield near Paris, he was asked the inevitable question, "How did you manage it?"

Lindberg responded, "It was easy. I did it alone."

How times change. Lindberg represents the vanishing American in a society becoming more complex and interdependent. Much as we admire the "do-it-yourself" spirit, youth of this generation find little they can do completely by themselves.

Someone else builds the house where we live, grows the food we eat, or makes the laws we obey. Youth can too easily get the feeling that they've entered the world scene too late to become leaders or doers. Too often the average person winds up pushing buttons in a factory or office. There's not much creativity or future doing that.

Beyond that feeling of uselessness which is pushed upon us is yet a greater danger. With so little to do by ourselves, we forget that some things like spiritual decisions must be "do-it-yourself" projects.

High in this category is a personal acceptance of God's plan for our life. He has already accomplished and planned everything necessary for our present joy and future salvation, but the rest is up to us. No parent or preacher can make spiritual decisions on behalf of any young person. There comes a time when each person must choose how he or she will relate personally to God.

For most people the thrill of sports comes only as a spectator along the sidelines. With God we can't just be an observer. We're involved on the playing field. When the ball comes to us, then it's our move!

Our legal system allows children of minority ages protection under the guardianship of parents. A ten-year-old child can't be jailed for nonpayment of debts or directly sued in civil courts. Even certain criminal acts are handled with special care in juvenile courts. But, sooner or later, the law declares the child must be treated with equality as an adult rather than a child. From then on the child stands alone before the law. God has a similar plan described as the age of accountability. Spiritually, we reach a stage in life when we go it alone with God.

A pastor's child examined a soul-winner's tract in his father's office. He already knew much about spiritual matters, but at age eight he had not yet accepted Jesus as Savior. Before his dad could return, he simply followed the directions for eternal life. He was saved. When his Sunday School teacher later asked how he was saved, he replied, "It was easy. I did it alone with Jesus."

Stewardship Sunday

Plan Ahead

Cast your bread upon the waters,/for you will find it after many days (Eccl. 11:1).

In 1981 Patricia West of Naples, Florida learned from her doctors just how special she is. Her blood contains some unusual antibodies found in only one of every five thousand persons.

Since nineteen out of twenty people are unable or unwilling to donate blood, her blood is for practical purposes one in one hundred thousand. That poses a critical problem for an otherwise routine procedure like a transfusion.

Would she be willing to donate some of her rare blood in case someone needed it? Some stranger's life might depend upon it. She would. And she did.

Later Mrs. West moved from Florida to Michigan. Then she hemorrhaged following a simple surgery. Her life hung in the balance.

Her doctors frantically searched for compatible blood. None was available. In desperation they called the National Rare Donor Registry whose computers located the blood in Florida. Doctors had no doubt that this blood in a freezer of the Edison Blood Bank would be compatible with the patient. It was Pat's own blood!

Virginia Parsons, director of the blood bank, said the standard shelf like of frozen blood is three years. "But very, very rare units like this" are kept for seven or eight years.

It was packed in dry ice and sent across the country on a lifesaving mission. Patricia West lives today because two years ago she was willing to give her own blood![1]

Life is like that. What we hoard and try to keep as treasure somehow gets away. What we give away so often comes back to bless our own lives many times beyond the original amount given.

Call it boomerang of blessings or just old-fashioned stewardship. But it's true. "Give, and it will be given to you; good measure, pressed down, shaken together, running over, will be put into your lap. For the measure you give will be the measure you get back" (Luke 6:38).

Note

1. *Dallas Morning News,* Apr. 16, 1983.

Back-to-School Day

Books and Bodies

> You are dust, and to dust you shall return (Gen. 3:19).
> Shall we descend together into the dust? (Job 17:16).

Back to school means back to the books. Not that we can ever escape the presence of books which are everywhere in life as well as school. Long ago Solomon observed "Of making many books there is no end" (Eccl. 12:12).

Books have always been popular, but modern technology took a long time providing Gutenberg's invention with enough paper to satisfy the world's writers. Only in the last hundred years has that fourteenth-century miracle been matched with inexpensive printing material which is turned into books.

Now everyone seems eager to make up for lost time. More books are pouring off printing presses each day now than the entire annual production a hundred years ago!

Books seem to have a permanent, eternal nature about them. We who are destined to return back to dust want to be remembered, but we don't trust florists to "say it with flowers." We want more than the poet's imagery of leaving behind our footprints in the sands of time.

In a practical sense, flowers fade and sands shift. We prefer to record our thoughts, values, and identity in the form of written words on paper. For self-expression and precise memories, paper and ink are an unbeatable combination. Wisdom in written form travels further and lasts longer than the brief threescore and ten years we are allotted in life.

Students of history and philosophy still read the thoughts of Socrates though he and his civilization perished long ago. Every writer dreams of being remembered in the distant future.

Whoa! Wait a minute. While everyone who is anyone seems to be writing (or having ghost-written) a book, consider one disturbing truth. In only twenty-five or thirty years today's books will have yellowing pages too brittle to touch!

The problem is our shortcut process dependent upon rosin and alum. Humidity, heat, light, and air pollution trigger this acid-soaked paper to literally eat itself. In only a generation or so our books are well on their way to becoming dust!

This is a major problem for libraries, historians, and courts. How can we possibly preserve important papers which are doomed to self-destruct? Europeans have recognized this danger sooner and are now switching their production to a safer but more expensive process. Americans are gradually following suit. Even then, the better paper will last only two hundred to three hundred years. What then?

The truth gradually emerges. Nothing in this physical world—from bodies to books—is guaranteed to last. Our books will join our bodies as dust. Our only hope is to be found in another book known as the "Lamb's book of life."

When we register our names and deeds through Jesus in that eternal record kept by God in heaven, then shall we be remembered by God

Himself. Let the body then turn to dust. Forget about earthly books destined for dust. We shall live forever!

Graduation

Standing Still

Be still, and know that I am God (Ps. 46:10).

An early television show featured a young man whose doctor offered no hope but an early death from a terminal disease. He kept the illness a secret, resolving to spend his remaining months in adventure as a young man always on the move.

It was an exciting series as he explored the depths of shark-infested waters, climbed mountains, and challenged dangerous criminals. Because he was going to die anyway, he took chances doing what others feared. The name of the program? *Run for Your Life.*

Many of us are like that young man running for life. Death is all around us. Despite the miracles of medical technology, the death rate remains the same. It's still at a constant 100 percent.

What are the driving forces in life? Hunger and thirst are strong physical needs as is the powerful biological drive of sexuality. The desire to succeed pushes us. We all need love and someone to love, but the ultimate preoccupation of life is an emotion—the fear of death.

Graduation and springtime seem far removed from death. It's the season of life and love, youth and beginnings when graduation robes, mortarboards, and tassels become popular. Like proud thoroughbreds straining at the gate, graduates are eager to run for life.

Centuries ago an obscure youth named Saul was chosen by God as the first king of Israel. Samuel, the aged prophet, informed the surprised teenager of that divine election and prepared him for his coronation that all Israel might know. What a commencement ceremony that would be!

We can imagine Saul's excitement as he anticipated good deeds that desperately needed doing *now.* There were enemies to be subdued, frontiers to be fortified, a nation to build, and a throne to secure. He would be a young man on the move.

Before Saul took the first step, however, he felt Samuel's heavy hand on his shoulder and heard some solemn advice. "But stand thou still a while, that I may shew thee the word of God" (1 Sam. 9:27, KJV).

Scripture doesn't tell us Saul's reaction, but he might have thought, *Man, you're crazy. Nobody ever gets anywhere just standing around. The world will pass me by. I've got to run in life!*

That's understandable. When we are young in both body and heart, when our feet are swift and troubles light, we want to tackle the world. Let's begin!

This reckless abandon, this confidence that we can solve the world's most vexing problems before dark seems presumptuous to older generations more cynical and less enthusiastic. Yet these youthful qualities are just what the troubled old world needs.

But Samuel offered a sensible caution to this truth. To be effective, youthful enthusiasm must be properly channeled. A course must be plotted with time taken to think about God. Slow down, stand still, and seek God's will. For a graduation unto a higher level, for a genuine commencement of life with purpose and perspective, then Samuel's advice is well worth heeding.

Senior Citizens' Day

Late Bloomers

And I am sure that he who began a good work in you will bring it to completion at the day of Jesus Christ (Phil. 1:6).

Are you a genius? You could demonstrate it by learning to play the harpsichord by age four, as Mozart did. By age five he was composing musical scores and performing before royalty at age six. That's budding genius.

If you're not a budding genius, cheer up. You can still be a late bloomer like Grandma Moses who led a quiet life until age seventy-six, when she began painting. She never had an art lesson, but with the maturity and discipline of later years she taught herself. Many of her most famous pictures are among the twenty-five done in her one-hundredth year.

But it was the original Moses who first qualified for a late-blooming award. Born to a Hebrew slave in Egypt, he was adopted by a Pharaoh's daughter and raised in the proverbial lap of luxury. Though a Hebrew, he was educated and trained as an Egyptian leader.

Who would he become? For his first forty years Moses struggled with his identity. Then one day his anger settled that question forever. He killed an Egyptian who had been cruelly treating Hebrew slaves. Had his life ended at age forty, Moses would have been remembered as a hotheaded murderer who fled in fear rather than face judgment.

The fugitive skipped the country. He eventually married and settled down to a lowly life tending his father-in-law's sheep. For the next forty years this gifted and educated man did little to improve himself or the world. Had his life ended at age eighty, Moses would have remained a failure, lost in the menial job market.

But God wasn't satisfied with Moses anymore than Moses was satisfied with himself. This Egyptian-born, Jewish peasant treated first to royal privilege and then to obscure poverty was still a chosen vessel of God. His eighty years of failure did not thwart the divine design. His reluctance might delay but not destroy God's plan.

After Moses had given up and felt he was too old to chase that elusive dream of freedom for his people, God at last got through to him. At the burning bush Moses fell on his face and into step with his Maker. The world was forever changed!

Those final forty years are history. Moses became a national deliverer, a social reformer, lawgiver, judge, and leader of God's people. All that in the last years of life!

Now what does this mean to us in modern America? We are growing older. Retirees, wrinkles, bald heads, and nursing homes now outnumber play swings and teenagers. Our baby boom will soon become ancient history in the "graying of America."

As we grow older, let's remember yesteryear's experience of Moses. We are never too old to be useful to God. Better to bloom late than never at all, but don't wait any longer. Be about God's business *now* with assurance that tomorrow's service in His kingdom will be even better than today's.

Senior Citizens' Day

Fruit in Old Age

> And let us not grow weary in well-doing, for in due season we shall reap, if we do not lose heart (Gal. 6:9).

They say aging is just another case of mind over matter. If you don't mind, then it doesn't matter!

Medical researchers are more discouraging. They report that physically you are "over the hill" by age twenty! For example, by age ten your ability to hear certain high sounds has already peaked. Normal hearing is best at age twenty. Unconditioned reflexes peak at age seventeen.

But take heart! Your productivity and creativity after age twenty need never stop because God has programmed into your body the possibility of something better than youth. It's called maturity.

We learn from our mistakes. This wonderful fact of life compensates for what we lose in youthful strength and makes possible the great productivity of later life. That's the promise of Psalm 92:14, "They still bring forth fruit in old age."

Many have proven this true. Before he was thirty the gifted and energetic Albert Schweitzer had won international acclaim as a theologian, organist, and historian of music. Then he studied medicine, moved to French Equatorial Africa, and built a desperately needed hospital.

Did the famous missionary physician fade in the sunset with retirement? No, at age seventy-seven he was awarded the Nobel peace prize and used the thirty-three thousand dollar reward to finance an ambitious expansion program of his hospital. His later ministry then included a leper colony and other accomplishments until death at age ninety.

Pablo Casals was still giving cello concerts at eighty-eight. At the same age the famous painter Michelangelo enjoyed drafting excellent architectural plans for great cathedrals which stand yet today as monuments not only to his eternal God but also to the accomplishments of an aging giant.

Tennyson was eighty-three when he penned his immortal poem, "The Crossing of the Bar." An eighty-two-year young Winston Churchill wrote, *A History of the English-Speaking People.*

Benjamin Franklin, a man of many abilities, could write, print, and invent. He was also a gifted linguist, orator, foreign diplomat, and government servant who never retired. After a long career of distinction, Franklin made his most enduring gift to our country. With tact and wisdom he moderated the compromise that led to the adoption of our American Constitution. He was then eighty-one.

There is no physical or spiritual law against productivity or achievement in the latter years. While the body and mind must gracefully submit to some changes in pace, the fruit-bearing years need never cease entirely. "And as your days, so shall your strength be" (Deut. 33:25).

In the first psalm a righteous believer is described as a tree

> that yields its fruit in its season,
> and its leaf does not wither.
> In all that he does, he prospers (v. 3).

Jesus continued that theme with the promise of much fruit. "By this my Father is glorified, that you bear much fruit, and so prove to be my disciple" (John 15:8).

Can you find any age restrictions in these Scriptures? Of course not.

So if you are feeling your corns nowadays more than your oats, don't worry! Stay alive, alert, and active. You never become too old to produce fruit for God.

3

Celebrations of Daily Living

Problems Or Possibilities

All things are possible to him who believes (Mark 9:23).

A little ditty describes a carpenter who could not see. "Now let me see," said the blind man. "So he picked up the hammer and saw!"

Some people might as well be blind. They always see problems instead of possibilities.

The greatest Old Testament event which molded God's people was a trip the Hebrew people took out of Egyptian slavery. Following those dramatic miracles, no one doubted God's deliverance through Moses. Every day was miracle day with manna and quail falling from the sky to provide their daily food. They were led by a strange pillar of cloud by day and fire by night toward the Promised Land flowing with milk and honey!

Then they arrived. God commanded them to possess their dream, so twelve spies were sent into the land to gather facts and formulate plans. They returned with tales of a truly prosperous land and brought back luscious fruit as positive proof.

But the scouts also returned with some negative notions. They were awed by fortified cities and dwarfed by giants beside whom "we seemed to ourselves like grasshoppers" (Num. 13:33).

That discouraging report caused their hearts to melt. They refused to enter the land, so God condemned them to death in the desert. For nearly forty years those people wandered aimlessly in the wilderness until the fainthearted generation died.

Then God raised up for Himself a new generation more excited about the possibilities than the problems of the Promised Land. They marched into the face of fear and adversity trusting God to give them victory. He did!

Both generations have many descendants alive today. Some say, "It can never be done." Others say, "Stand aside! We'll show you how!"

Problems or possibilities—which do you see? That depends upon whether you trust only what you can see. Shortsighted realism whispers into your ear, "You don't stand a chance. The devil has this world under his control, so better not be hardheaded. Coast along with the crowd. Let someone else take the risks of faith."

But faith sees beyond the problem to a deeper truth and a higher power. Sometimes we can only muddle through the darkness not sure of our directions. While we may wonder about the *where,* we need never worry about the *who.* We take a step at a time with God.

A desperate father brought his afflicted son to Jesus. The boy often fell into spastic seizures, foaming at the mouth and rolling about. The disciples had tried to help, but they could not. Then the father begged Jesus, "But if you can do anything, have pity on us and help us."

That's quite a problem. Not the illness but the father's half faith. With the Great Physician, healing was only a miracle away. Jesus wanted first to help the father, His disciples, the bystanders, and us later readers to increase faith beyond problem to possibility.

"If you can! All things are possible to him who believes." There's the formula of faith from the lips of our Lord for all generations. Focus upon Jesus and believe in Him to whom all things are possible.

Warts And All

For the Lord sees not as man sees; man looks on the outward appearance, but the Lord looks on the heart (1 Sam. 16:7).

"Mirror, mirror on the wall, am I beautiful, warts and all?" If the mirror seems to mock you in silence, don't fret. Don't worry if your ears are too big, your legs too short, or your nose too long.

Be glad that you are different. God planned it that way. The Master Designer refuses to mass produce His highest creation. No cheap replicas for God! Every person is an original.

But not an original mistake, since God makes no mistakes. He meant you to look just like you are, an original creation in His own image.

So accept yourself. Let plastic surgeons serve accident victims or other extreme cases, but not for casual changes in the name of vanity.

A prospective appointed for a major government position appeared before a Senate committee for confirmation. He answered every question with total honesty. Reporters later asked him about the results. With a big grin he said. "They took me—warts and all!"

Which reminds us of a beloved President. When Abraham Lincoln was elected to our nation's highest office, a photographer came for an official portrait. It turned out too well. Family and friends all agreed that the unsightly wart on Lincoln's face should be erased on the negative. Lincoln steadfastly refused on the grounds that his photograph had to be honest.

Amen! That honest reflection, warts and all, has become one of our most cherished, presidential profiles. Lincoln had the courage to be himself. He concentrated upon honest character rather than cover-up cosmetics.

Have you ever noticed how personal descriptions in the New Testament differ from those in the Old Testament? In the older era physical features were emphasized in detail. Saul was "a handsome young man" a head taller than others while David was "ruddy, and had beautiful eyes, and was handsome" (1 Sam. 9:2; 16:12).

Christ so changed people's values that the New Testament reflects a better standard. The outside is not as important as the inside. Spiritual qualities outshine the physical.

We are told about the clothing John the Baptist wore, the food he ate, how he acted, and what he preached. We even know about his doubts but nothing at all concerning his physical appearance. Ditto for the twelve, the first deacons, and even Paul, missionary to the Gentiles. Most incredible, no one bothered to describe any physical features of Jesus. Was he tall, short, or thin? What type nose? What size hands or feet?

God had a purpose for that silence. We are not to judge others by outside appearance, a truth taught but seldom practiced in the Old Testament. God is just as unhappy with beauty contests as with racial prejudice. Any judgment or opinion based upon one's body is wrong. That includes the so-called "positive prejudices" for beautiful women who impress us or the tall men before whom we may stand in awe.

Now can you imagine how unfair we could be knowing that Jesus was tall or his mother possessed certain physical traits of desired beauty? Prejudice is bad enough now without having people base their unholy beliefs upon the body of Jesus. No telling what kind of extremes could follow. Had Jesus been described as bowlegged and hollow-eyed, doubtless those characteristics would have been viewed today as standards or norms for achievement. All true saints *must* be bowlegged and hollow-eyed!

How wonderful that with God we are loved no matter how we look—and that includes knock-knees, buck teeth, and flat feet! If only everyone could be satisfied that God makes no mistakes and loves all His original creations equally. The real test of character and beauty is within our hearts.

Struggle and Strength

No temptation has overtaken you that is not common to man. God is faithful, and he will not let you be tempted beyond your strength, but with the temptation will also provide the way of escape, that you may be able to endure it (1 Cor. 10:13).

So you have it rough? Well, you're not the only one. Consider this case.

In 1820 a six-week-old baby caught a cold which settled in her eyes. It was still no serious matter until a country doctor prescribed the wrong drops which caused blindness. Five years later a famous specialist examined her and concluded, "Poor little blind girl!" She had no hope for sight.

Others with less courage would have given up. Not Fanny J. Crosby. Instead of being consumed with self-pity, the little girl accepted the medical verdict as a challenge. She would not be isolated by her blindness.

At age fifteen Fanny entered an institution for the blind to be trained as a typist which her parents felt would at least provide her an income. She preferred writing and was soon dictating poetry for the other students to type!

What Fanny could not see with her eyes, she felt with her spirit and expressed with her pen. Biographers have suggested the lady who lived in darkness could sense the very heartbeat of the God of light. Over eight thousand hymns and sacred songs flowed from her searching soul. The struggles of Fanny Crosby have provided spiritual strength for generations who have found in her sentiment and song the words to praise God.

Now what about your struggles and strengths? You are probably not blind, but like everyone else you have your own problems. Remember this. Your pain is never unique or one of a kind. Somewhere others are suffering the same way and have learned to triumph over trial.

Paul offered wise counsel in 1 Corinthians 10:13. "No temptation has overtaken you that is not common to man."

Where do we get the idea that we deserve privileged treatment even from Satan? The same old sufferings and sins which plague others will do quite nicely for the devil's purpose toward us. He does not need to serve us some special type of exotic temptation when the common type can trip us so easily. Indeed, the verse ensures us that we will not be tempted by anything but ordinary, human sins.

Same struggle, same strength. If we are so much alike, why do some fail in the face of adversity while others flourish? The difference is a matter of choice. God gives us freedom to respond in a way to make life better or worse.

Like Fanny Crosby, you can choose whether your problems will make or break you. You can grieve or you can grow. You can turn your buffetings into blessings. It's your choice!

Gold Fever

> Therefore let anyone who thinks that he stands take heed lest he fall (1 Cor. 10:12).

"Gold is where you find it," and Albert Strelow knew it was so. He had grown up hearing stories about men who dropped everything for the California gold rush in 1849. It was common knowledge that most gold prospectors died penniless.

The senior Strelow wasn't the kind of man who gave in to capricious whims. Young Albert was raised by a father who believed in hard work rather than risky chance.

In those days so many neighbors were bitten by the gold bug and

Detroit nearly failed. The frontier city depended upon immigrants for their lumber-based economy. Even before the gold rush Detroit had a shortage of laborers to clear the forests.

Without an adequate supply of lumber, the shipbuilding industry suffered. Ditto for the manufacture of wagons, railroad cars, and furniture. Yet by the end of the century this same depressed industry based upon Michigan's lumber had generated a billion dollars more value than all of California's gold!

Yes, Strelow understood that more fortunes are earned by hard work and local resources than by get-rich-quick schemes. He also realized that Michigan's great deposits of copper and coal could some day make Detroit a manufacturing center.

An inventor named Henry Ford had the same idea. Ford claimed he could profitably produce the horseless carriage in Detroit. After several false starts resulting in heavy losses for local banks, Ford was ready to try again. Strelow plunked down his life savings of five thousand dollars and invited Ford to build the first Model A in Strelow's backyard barn.

Within months the venture succeeded. Here was an investment better than gold. In three years Strelow's share of the new company had increased in value seven times over. The future was bright.

Then in 1906 Strelow heard a rumor. A small group of smart men had a sure thing in a Canadian gold mine. Here was a chance to make millions. Strelow wavered. Then he bit. Selling his five thousand shares of Ford stock for thirty-five thousand dollars profit, he gambled it all on gold.

Strelow lost everything. What happened to his original shares of Ford stock? Thirteen years later in 1919 that same stock sold for thirteen million dollars! Imagine what it's worth today.

Like Strelow, we know better than fall victim to some common sins. We avoid the temptations many times. Then later, in a moment of weakness, we take the bait and get caught.

Satan never gives up. We must be wary even of those temptations where we think we stand the strongest. Take heed!

Knowing the Author

Wherefore seeing we also are compassed about with so great a cloud of witnesses, let us lay aside every weight, and the sin which doth so easily beset us, and let us run with patience the race that is set before us, Looking unto Jesus the author and finisher of our faith (Heb. 12:1-2, KJV).

Upon graduation from college a young lady landed a dream job. She was at last a librarian. All her life this lover of books looked forward to the day when she could read, examine, and catalog them.

During this daily routine she processed a new book without being the least bit impressed. While some titles or subjects offered the promise of excitement, this one looked like a boring book.

Then one day the woman with her dream job met her dream man. With only a glance and a greeting the two had fallen madly in love. On their first date she mentioned that somehow his name sounded familiar. Then she remembered. "We have a book in our library written by someone with the same name."

The young man's face brightened as he replied, "That's no coincidence. I wrote that book."

When she arrived home that night, she wasted no time before secretly returning to the closed library. With her pass key and flashlight she had no trouble finding the little volume. Then she took it home and stayed up reading until 3:00 AM This was the most fascinating book she had ever read!

What made the difference between dull and delightful? The book hadn't changed. She had, because she had met the author.

The Bible is an interesting book of history, poetry, and inspiration. As a literary masterpiece it attracts attention, invites interest, and will always be a bestseller.

But what a difference knowing the Author can make! When people meet God, then His Word becomes a treasured book indeed.

Support System

For no other foundation can any one lay than that which is laid, which is Jesus Christ (1 Cor. 3:11).

Modern architecture is forever indebted to Sir Christopher Wren who rebuilt much of London after the disastrous fire of 1666. His legacy includes more than fifty churches in a variety of graceful styles.

Wren's striking design of St. Paul's Cathedral established him as the world's leading architect. Unfortunately, that fame led jealous rivals to criticize his work all the more.

The capable artist ignored his critics to explore new techniques. Wren designed a massive dome supported by a single column. The uproar was predictable. Surely this church would crumble! He must add additional supports.

Wren held firm. He was confident in his work, but it was one of the few battles he was destined to lose. Amid much political intrigue, the prominent designer was forced to add two more pillars.

The controversy faded and was forgotten. Half a century later the dome needed repainting, so workmen assembled scaffolds. Were they ever surprised! The two added pillars were never connected to the roof. Short by two feet, they served as a decoration or adornment for appearance only.

Wren had the last word. His ability and the completed project were both vindicated. Just one support was enough to bear all that weight.

Is your own life that secure? During the Christmas season family and friends gather to exchange gifts and express love. We need that kind of a support system to keep the world from falling in on us. It's a sad season to spend alone. Family, friends, career, and physical comforts help us feel secure—but for how long?

Measured in light of eternity, human relationships serve a purpose limited to earth. However desirable now, they won't provide entry into heaven. Anyone depending upon family name or human connections will find these temporary supports as useless as Wren's fake columns.

The only real foundation in life is Jesus Christ. He is not an option but a necessity; not an extra decoration on the tree of life but the basic requirement for eternal life. Jesus is our pillar of power now and forever.

> Even to your old age I am He,
> and to gray hairs I will carry you.
> I have made, and I will bear;
> I will carry and will save (Isa. 46:4).

Made for a Master

> Whatever good anyone does, he will receive the same again from the Lord, whether he is slave or free. Masters, do the same to them, and forbear threatening, knowing that he who is both their Master and yours is in heaven (Eph. 6:8-9).

Diogenes failed in his first search. The Greek philosopher, best remembered for carrying his lamp in search of an honest man, never really found one. Fortunately, he succeeded in a more urgent quest. This second search began unwittingly after he booked passage on an ill-fated ship later captured by pirates. Along with the other surviving passengers and crew, Diogenes found himself on the slave market being pushed and prodded by prospective purchasers.

A slave trader correctly guessed that Diogenes was no field hand. Did he have a useful trade? The prisoner replied that he was no tradesman or skilled laborer. His only trade was being a governor or leader of men. Thus, Diogenes concluded, "I would like to be sold to a man who needs a master."

And he was. A wealthy merchant bought Diogenes to tutor his sons and become adviser-ruler of his household. Diogenes again became the master.

Diogenes was an astute observer of human nature. Finding a man in need of a master is far easier than the search for an honest man.

I'm in need of a master. Aren't we all? But not just another human master who forms a tyrannical cult. Free people need a Master out of this world. Diogenes and his kin have to fall in line with the rest of us mere mortals seeking more than any worldly person can offer.

Only Jesus can satisfy our search for a sufficient Savior and living Lord. He's the Master twice named by the terrified disciples when their boat filled with water and appeared to be sinking. Several of these men were professional fishermen familiar with this lake but not with a storm that fierce. In desperation they turned to Jesus, who was asleep.

What an incredible demonstration of perfect peace! Anyone who could gently rest in that moment of crisis was indeed God—or a man so foolish he didn't understand danger. They would soon discover the real Jesus.

> "Master, Master, we are perishing!" And he awoke and rebuked the wind and the raging waves; and they ceased, and there was a calm. He said to them, "Where is your faith?" And they were afraid, and they marveled, saying to one another, "Who then is this, that he commands even wind and water, and they obey him" (Luke 8:24-25)?

Ever notice how people answer their own questions? "Master, Master," they cried. They were right the first time. Jesus proved indeed to be a Master with power over nature. Before such a great God we all stand with clay feet and equal worth. No person on earth can equal our Master in heaven! We are made for that kind of Master.

Instant Saints

> Therefore, my beloved brethren, be steadfast, immovable, always abounding in the work of the Lord, knowing that in the Lord your labor is not in vain. (1 Cor. 15:58).

Americans are in a hurry. The faster the better. That's why instant potatoes outsell minute rice and the super kind of glues are the most sensational sellers of all. Commercials show how only one drop produces a bond strong enough to support the weight of an automobile, but few people buy that product for its power. We seek speed more than strength. No need to wait for it to dry. Just touch and the job is done. That's the American way!

As usual, the marketplace has its mirror or reflection in religion where instant sainthood is the big attraction. Books, magazines, television interviews, and convention programs highlight the dramatic testimonies of celebrities who have found Christ. Their impact (or profitability to those who market Christianity) is measurable to any businessman. It's not previous popularity, present fame, or future ability to communicate God's love but rather how sordid the sinner before his salvation.

One must be careful to avoid the Pharisaic attitude of resenting these new converts, so let us welcome them. They are an inspiration to this era of spiritual decline as we witness God at work through changed lives. Praise the Lord!

But now a word of caution. Instant saints born of overnight miracles ought to be heard gladly, but they can't be so soon mature in the faith they so long spurned. We Christians may be curious, but we have no right to expect them to preach or publish immediate wisdom beyond this limited experience of conversion.

What happens when they make mistakes and commit sins (as we

all inevitably do) under the glare of the spotlight? It's all too public. Even the Christian crowd is critical and fickle, quick to dump fallen stars who fail to live up to the high standards of the cross.

Is there no middle ground? Their testimonies ought to be heard, but the whirlwind speaking tours and hastily published biographies (usually ghost-written) can wait. Surely these babes in Christ can be given time to grow before we thrust them on stage as spiritual experts.

A patient cured by dramatic surgery may have some inside perspective but not enough to perform that same surgical procedure on others. It takes time to see the experience in perspective and how God worked that miracle using others. It's only later that most postoperative patients get around to realizing that their successful surgery involved the teamwork of an entire hospital staff.

In the same way a new convert often overlooks the support system of God's church which surely had some part in his or her salvation and deserves a place in that follow-up growth. He needs to channel his newfound spiritual energies into a local group of believers where more prayers are offered for others yet unsaved. They grow and he grows.

The conversion experience of an adult requires a follow-up period of growth and search for perspective. When Saul met Jesus on the dusty Damascus road, he soon retired to a wilderness retreat for three years. He needed time to evaluate and seek God's will instead of plunging into a new life-style on the celebrity circuit before packed houses of cheering Christians.

A better way is offered by the local church. Here the convert can join God's rank and file working beside faithful but not famous servants who have given lifetime service to his army. Call them plodders if you wish, but those faithful followers who worship every Sunday and visit each Thursday night are the real heroes. They kept the church doors open all those years while the recent converts went their own worldly ways.

Following a key victory for Napoleon's army, his general staff approached him concerning the brave and resourceful actions of a young officer who had won the day. They recommended an immediate reward in the form of a field promotion. The Little General was not satisfied.

"That's fine," said Napoleon, "but why not wait until the next battle and see if he is really solid?" As it turned out, the popular young leader was not nearly so resourceful as everyone thought. In his next assignment he failed miserably. While nothing was said further, Napoleon's staff was thankful they hadn't thrust the young man into a prominent position of magnified danger. It was best to let him grow.

The Starting Line

> Because, if you confess with your lips that Jesus is Lord and believe in your heart that God raised him from the dead, you will be saved. For man believes with his heart and so is justified, and he confesses with his lips and so is saved. (Rom. 10:9-10).

Talk about a great race! When Congress decided to open the Oklahoma territory for homesteading, over fifty thousand hopeful settlers crowded into a starting line stretching over twenty-five miles wide.

The great giveaway brought an unprecedented land boom. Wagonloads of prospective settlers ("Boomers") rolled in from all over the country. For three days US cavalry troops kept the excited participants at bay.

Finally at high noon on April 23, 1889, starting cannons sounded simultaneously for miles along the border. The troops retreated as thousands of Boomers rushed deep into the territory seeking the best land to claim.

Some key areas had already been surveyed and platted for cities. Before the day was over a stretch of prairie became a vibrant tent city of ten thousand known as Oklahoma City.

Businesses like banks and general stores operated from the first day in wagons. The second day they moved into tents while waiting for permanent buildings to be erected within weeks.

What was necessary to claim this free land? Recording fees were expected, but the most important requirement was being there to take possession.

No property was available by proxy or for absentee landowners. Settlers had to be physically present to make their claims.

Incidentally, fast Boomers in the lead discovered some sneaky settlers had slipped in early. They had hidden in gullies and woods listening for the stampede so they could jump out in front. They were the original "Sooners."

The Oklahoma run is now history, but God still has places reserved in heaven. In a spiritual sense, earth is the starting line for heaven.

Strange, but some people never give God much attention. They act as if heaven can wait or that their future is automatically assured. It's not.

If you're going to heaven, you have to start somewhere. Unless you line up and begin, you are a guaranteed loser.

Yet everyone wins who starts out on this road to life. Salvation is a gift free and clear. God has provided everything.

Our only requirement is to begin the journey in faith. The starting line is called belief, faith, or trust.

We all begin the same way. The process involves repentance and a new birth from above. But it must start somewhere with a personal decision to begin in faith.

Whose Are You?

> You are not your own; you were bought with a price. So glorify God in your body (1 Cor. 6:19-20).

Just *who* are you, anyway? One way to answer that point-blank question of identity is in possessive terms of *whose* you are.

For example, names reflect a sense of ownership or belonging. The surname indicates family to whom we are born or given in marriage. That's a perspective of possession.

When Mrs. Smith signs her name with that title, she emphasizes how she belongs to Mr. Smith. In casual conversation Mr. Smith refers to Mrs. Smith as "*my* wife."

And what about children? While they have certain constitutional rights in their minor years, they must nevertheless legally "belong" to an adult parent or guardian. It's the law.

Perhaps you wish to donate your body to medical science. You can declare your intentions now. Yet, no matter how many papers you may sign, the agreement is not legally binding.

Our laws decree that you have only a temporary ownership of your own body. Upon your death that body belongs to the surviving marriage mate or nearest of kin. The decision which counts is theirs, not yours.

In life and in death we belong to others. Yet that is a nice feeling. For all our fuss about freedom and independence, we can't escape this deep human need to belong.

You can belong to a union, a country club, or even a church; take your pick of many invitations, but the only ultimate sense of belonging rests in God.

The Bible says we are created in the image of God. Though we may rebel and go our own way, the Original Maker never gave us up.

In a dramatic death on the cross, God through Jesus Christ provided a plan for redemption. He paid the ultimate price for our sin. He who was sinless offered His own life in payment for our sins.

The choice is ours to become double-possessed—once by original creation and then finally through this spiritual option of being bought back by God. There's never an identity crisis with those who then know whose they are.

So whose are you? When you belong to Jesus, that question is settled once and forever. He who bought you with a price—that terrible price paid in blood of a sinless Savior—can keep you safe and secure. No doubt about that.

"My sheep hear my voice, and I know them, and they follow me; and I give them eternal life, and they shall never perish, and no one shall snatch them out of my hand" (John 10:27-28).

Time Bomb

Be angry but do not sin. Do not let the sun go down on your anger. Let all bitterness and wrath and anger and clamor and slander be put away from you, with all malice, and be kind to one another, tender-hearted, forgiving one another, as God in Christ forgave you (Eph. 4:26, 31-32).

When do the explosive echoes of World War II cease? Ask the John Stanley family of Middleboro, Massachusetts who survived a recent 1983 reminder of that grim war.

Their evening began innocently enough when Mr. Stanley put a log on the fire. Then came the blast which left a two-inch gash in the fireplace screen and another hole in the ceiling. Fortunately, no one was hurt.

So how can a stick of firewood be connected with a war forty years past? The wood was cut on the site of a munitions testing range.

Apparently a live shell from an antiaircraft gun had been embedded in a tree all this time. The twenty millimeter explosive had lost none of its power originally packed in the three-inch long by five-eighths-inch-wide shell.

Demolition experts warn us that the older the explosive, the more unstable and dangerous it becomes. They shudder at the thought of thousands of war souvenirs accidentally exploding in homes across America. Every unexploded shell is a ticking time bomb.

Unexploded shells aren't the only danger lurking in life. Emotions like anger, hate, and hostility can be just as explosive when not handled correctly.

How do you deal with these negative forces in your life? Some people don't. When betrayed by a friend or deeply hurt by an acquaintance, they try to ignore it. We may even consider them strong for seeming to forget the matter.

Then years later some small straw breaks the camel's back. They blow up over nothing. In extreme cases mild-mannered people become raving maniacs.

More typical is the grudge kept alive but under control just below the surface. The person wronged doesn't get mad, but just waits to get even.

Of course, getting even never works out even. No amount of wrong can make something right. The time bomb just changes into an ugly cancer and gets worse as it spreads to other people.

Jesus taught forgiveness as the best way to defuse explosive emotions. To forgive someone is like releasing a prisoner from jail. Later you discover that the prisoner set free is you!

Eternal Winner

> Rejoice and be glad, for your reward is great in heaven, for so men persecuted the prophets who were before you (Matt. 5:12).

Don't look now, but you may have already won a sweepstakes drawing worth thousands of dollars. Other possible winnings include cars, vacations, or at least a big discount off something you weren't planning to buy soon. All you need do is return the form and await breathlessly your reward.

So what's the gimmick? It's a double appeal of getting something for nothing and becoming a winner.

From every direction we are bombarded with this selfish combination. Let everyone else be last. YOU can be *Number One.* Leave the losers behind.

Of course, it's all part of a sales pitch. If this bothers you, don't blame it on the advertisers. They do not want to irritate us or drive us away, but they know what sells. To introduce us to their new products, they use the ideas we like best.

If you want to examine the basic attitudes of America, study our advertising. This industry is a mirror which reflects our real values.

We Americans are more than just competitive. We are obsessed with winning. Witness the little leagues where parents shout obscenities at hapless officials. The message is clear. Forget fairness. Win at any cost!

Few men in sports have been more admired than Vince Lombardi, late coach of the Green Bay Packers. What was his philosophy? "Winning isn't everything. Winning is the only thing!"

Some positive-minded people like to package the good news of Jesus in one exciting sentence: "Be a winner with Jesus." They have a point, but Jesus also talked about taking life's lowest place, of the narrow gate, and where the way is hard.

Sometimes we must turn the other cheek to be blessed when people revile, persecute, and utter all kinds of evil against us falsely. In that case, we can still rejoice for our reward is great in heaven, if not on earth.

Virtue is not always rewarded here on earth. Godly men from Abel to Abraham and Job to Jeremiah were persecuted for their righteousness. Many times they appeared to be life's big losers. But earthly competition is not complete until the heavenly rewards are distributed to the eternal winners.

Who To Trust?

> It is better to trust in the Lord than to put confidence in man. Trust in the Lord with all thine heart; and lean not unto thine own understanding (Ps. 118:8; Prov. 3:5, KJV).

When dealing in big bucks, common sense seeks to reduce risk where possible. No wonder the big corporations hire outside consultants who help them make the expensive decisions.

Market researchers have developed sophisticated (and very expensive) techniques to eliminate guesswork. They can supposedly predict whether a product—anything from fast food to Hollywood films—will sell.

But even the pros can be wrong. Ask the folks at Twentieth-Century Fox who heard some bad news in 1976. Halfway through production of a costly movie, consultants warned that the plot was weak and childish.

Besides that, the robots featured in the film should be taken out. People just don't like robots.

The movie title was also suspect because it included the word *war*. That word alone would kill this movie because peace lovers would oppose it.

The executives agonized over this expensive research. Finally they tossed it in the trash can, released *Star Wars* and grossed $525 million!

Ashley Boone, the vice-president who made that critical decision, says: "Thank God, we threw out the research." His obvious relief sounds as if someone had appealed for Divine guidance.

We doubt it, but that's not a bad idea. The good Lord knows how hard it is for us to live by faith. Trust doesn't come easy for us.

Who can you trust? A restaurant sign proclaims, "In God We Trust." A second line below says in smaller print, "Everyone else pays cash."

A proverb reminds us: "Trust in man and he will let you down. Trust in God and He will lift you up."

Good advice! The next time you have a major decision, pray about it. Trust God for wisdom from above.

> Thou dost keep him in perfect peace,
> whose mind is stayed on thee,
> because he trusts in thee (Isa. 26:3).

Life Without Limits

I came that they may have life, and have it abundantly (John 10:10).

After years of suffering without silence, the hypochrondriac finally died. He was 102 years old. On his tombstone they dutifully engraved his last words: "I Told You I Was Sick!"

Florence Nightingale would have understood that chronic complainer, but not from her professional perspective as the mother of modern nursing. Practitioners of the medical arts are notoriously hard on patients with imagined illnesses.

Florence was a compassionate soul, but she had more personal reasons for identifying with hypochondriacs. The Lady of the Lamp was herself a sister in suffering for thrill of it.

While yet a young woman she had accomplished much in her goal of better treatment for the sick. The strong-willed nurse followed her nation's soldiers off to battle in the Crimean War. She ministered effectively. Hospitals were being reformed according to her demands.

When Florence returned to England in 1856, she confided to friends that her own life "hung by a thread." It was her heart. So only thirty-six years of age, the famous nurse took to bed. Surely her condition was terminal.

Her self-diagnosis was proven correct when Florence later died of apparent heart failure. Only her timing was off. She waited in bed for fifty-four years before dying at age ninety![1]

Forence Nightingale quit too soon. Her career was cut short, not by death or disease but by her own self-imposed restrictions. She cheated herself out of an abundant life offered by God.

Not everyone can have robust health in our world, but health or sickness aren't the problem. Some who are bedridden live the fullest and happiest lives. They agree with Paul. "Not that I complain of want; for I have learned, in whatever state I am, to be content" (Phil. 4:11). That's life without limits, the abundant life provided only through Jesus Christ.

Note

1. Irving Wallace, *The Book of Lists, No. 2* (New York: William Morrow and Co., 1980), p. 368.

Invisible Support

Blessed be the God and Father of our Lord Jesus Christ! By his great mercy we have been born anew to a living hope through the resurrection of Jesus Christ from the dead (1 Pet. 1:3).

"You never meet an atheist in a war-time foxhole!" Or so they say. Perhaps you know an exception. It's possible that a nonbeliever might have no doubts in the face of death.

Then again, a blind man about to stumble over a rock and down a cliff might not be afraid either. In that case, ignorance could be mistaken for courage.

One of Christianity's most outspoken critics was Francois Marie Arouet better known by his pen name, Voltaire. The privileged son born to an aristocratic family and educated in the best Jesuit schools rebelled against religion controlled by a corrupt church. Today we suspect Voltaire was more against that corruption than against God.

The playwright, poet, and philosopher is best remembered today as a foe of God. His rallying cry was "Ecrasez l'infame" ("Crush the evil thing"), referring to religious superstition.

Was Voltaire an atheist? Hardly. Once when he was asked about God, he replied: "We nod but do not speak."

That's not much of a faith for death or other life crises. But at least Voltaire did not deny God's existence like an American father who had reared his son in atheism. Together they become constant critics of Christianity.

Finally, the older man lay dying. Plagued by doubts, he asked his strong son: "Do you think we've made a mistake?"

The son choked back tears, trying to remain firm in the face of death. "Don't give in to those thoughts, Dad. Hold on. Please hold on."

"That's just it, Son. There's nothing for me to hold on to."

And that is the ultimate problem with atheism. This empty philosophy offers no invisible means of support!

But then atheism has never done anything positive for people. Rather than belief that builds up, it tears down. A negative belief in nothing accomplishes nothing.

Have you ever heard of an Atheistic Memorial Hospital or a University of Atheism? Of course not. They don't build orphanages for homeless children or minister to the poor, either.

But it is in death's dark hour that atheism's cruel self-ignorance costs the most. There's nothing left then to hold onto through the valley of the shadow of death.

During his last months Voltaire weakened in the grip of a fatal illness. How did he respond? Not belligerently. God's most prominent foe sent for the parish priest! He was beaten and would surrender.

In a letter dictated on his deathbed, the intellectual giant tried to atone for living apart from God for eighty-four years. "I did confess to the Reverend Rector of Sulpice that if it pleased God to dispose of me, I would die in the church in which I was born. Hoping that the Divine mercy will pardon my faults, I sign myself . . . Voltaire."[1]

What made the difference? Why was Voltaire "hoping that the Divine mercy will pardon"? That "living hope" and "great mercy" (1 Pet. 1:3) was freely provided through the resurrection of Jesus. The philosopher finally claimed what God had promised all along.

In the end we must realize that only God holds power over death, and only Jesus has ever returned from the grave to be with us in our fear of the grave. We can hold on to God in Jesus because He promises to be present. "Yea, though I walk through the valley of the shadow of death, I will fear no evil: for thou are with me" (Ps. 23:4, KJV).

Note

1. Richard Bewes, "What Rocks Ardent Unbelievers?" *Eternity,* Sept., 1983, p. 67.

In the Family

Fear not, for I have redeemed you;
I have called you by name, you are mine.
When you pass through the waters I will be with you.
. . . For I am the Lord your God
. . . Because you are precious in my eyes,
and honored, and I love you (Isa. 43:1-4).

The curator of a major zoo tells how a distraught woman sought a new home in the zoo for her monkey. The cute little pet had attacked their six-month-old baby. For the infant it was a close brush with death.

Obviously the monkey was jealous of this newest household pet, but the woman couldn't believe it. "After all," she said, "the monkey often stood over the infant and smiled."

Poor misguided lady. She didn't know about threat grimaces by wild creatures. What she interpreted as a smile was a warning or challenge similar to a dog's growl. The monkey felt threatened by the child, so he challenged that unwelcome intruder.

Had the baby been a monkey, the danger could have been avoided by returning the "smile" for a standoff. Unfortunately, the pet assumed a lack of response meant cowardly submission. That was an open invitation to attack the newcomer in a crib.

This problem is not limited to cute monkeys or green-eyed monsters. The root of jealousy is a feeling of inferiority linked to fear. Insecure people are afraid and feel worthless.

A good news-bad news joke has the doctor reporting to his patient: "Good news! You don't have an inferiority complex after all. The bad news is that you don't have anything. You are just plain inferior!"

Not according to the Bible! We may be guilty sinners who fall short of God's glory, but inferiority is one feeling we don't have to be ashamed of. After all, we are made in the image of God. As the little boy said, "I'm OK because God don't make no junk!"

That is bad English but good theology. We are children of the King, of the Heavenly Father. The ancients said the Jews made terrible slaves because they were so secure and proud of their special relationship as God's people. They preferred death to slavery. Because God had dramatically rescued them so often from captivity, they understood only that they weren't born to be slaves.

We are not peasants or pawns in the power plays of this world. God has purpose and worth for every person. We are twice chosen as God's children, first by original creation (God's choice) and second by redemption (our choice). When we belong to Jesus through this double bond, we can find our proper place in His will.

Granted, some lean to the opposite extreme of thinking themselves better than others. Perverted perfectionism and snobbish elitism are just as wrong as constant shame and suicidal impulses. Avoid both extremes. Learn to live as a branch of the true vine in God's family.

> Abide in me, and I in you. As the branch cannot bear fruit by itself, unless it abides in the vine, neither can you, unless you abide in me. These things I have spoken to you, that my joy may be in you, and that your joy may be full (John 15:4,11).